French Connections

French Connections

Voices from the women's movement in France

Edited and translated by Claire Duchen

The University of Massachusetts Press Amherst, 1987

LC 86–11347

ISBN 0–87023–547–8 (cloth); 548–6 (pbk.)

Library of Congress Cataloging-in-Publication Data

French connections.

 Translated from the French.
 Bibliography: p.
 1. Feminism——France.   2. Women——France.
3. Lesbianism——France.   I. Duchen, Claire.
HQ1617.F74 1987   305.4′2′0944   86–11347
ISBN 0–87023–547–8
ISBN 0–87023–548–6 (pbk.)

Contents

Acknowledgements

The editor and publishers would like to thank the following people for permission to translate and publish the articles in this anthology:

Françoise Collin for *Au Revoir*; Christine Delphy for *Women's liberation: the tenth year* and for Eliane Viennot's *Feminism and political parties: the impossible union*; Editions Grasset for the extracts from Annie Leclerc's *Parole de Femme*; Colette Guillaumin for *The Question of Difference*; *Le Matin* newspaper for the interview between Catherine Clément and Antoinette Fouque; Françoise Pasquier for material from *La Revue d'en Face*; the authors of the *Letter to the Feminist Movement* and other radical lesbian tracts; the ex-*courant G.*

I was unable to locate the *Elles Voient Rouge* collective, which no longer exists.

All the authors received copies of the translation of their texts. I would like to thank them all for their corrections and their comments.

Notes on authors

Françoise Collin founded *les cahiers du Grif* in 1973, and is still its 'animator'. She has a doctorate in philosophy and teaches in Brussels, although she now lives in Paris. She has published essays and two novels with Gallimard and has contributed to several collective works. She hopes to put her numerous articles together in a collection soon.

Christine Delphy is a sociologist. She is best known for her work on class, gender and the family. She has been involved in the MLF since its beginning and her articles have been extremely influential in the development of radical feminist theory. Christine Delphy is a member of the *Nouvelles Questions Féministes* collective and was a founder member of *Questions Féministes*. A collection of her essays and articles in translation is published in the Explorations in Feminism series: *Close to Home*, translated and edited by Diana Leonard (1984).

Catherine Deudon has been involved in the MLF since October 1970, identifying mainly (but not only) with the *Féministes Révolutionnaires* group. She wrote (anonymously) for *Le Torchon Brûle*. In 1972, she co-founded the group *Gouines Rouges* (Red Dykes). Catherine Deudon participated in many events, demonstrations and publications of the MLF, including the occupation of the *librairie des femmes* in 1976, the 'sexisme ordinaire' section of the journal *les Temps Modernes*, and the group *féminisme et politique* (feminism and politics) in 1981. Since 1982, she has been employed at the Simone de Beauvoir audio-visual centre as a photographer.

Marie-Jo Dhavernas has a BA in philosophy, an MA in sociology and a PhD in history. She has been active in the MLF since 1972 and while she doesn't identify absolutely with any one 'current', she mostly participated in actions with radical feminists. She was in the editorial collective of *la Revue d'en Face* and wrote for the 'sexisme ordinaire' section of *les Temps Modernes*. She is particularly interested in a critique of naturalist ideology. She is working with Liliane Kandel on the relation of sexism and racism, and she organizes, with Rosi Braidotti, a seminar at the Collège de Philosophie in Paris.

Colette Guillaumin is a sociologist who is particularly interested in naturalist ideology. She was a member of the *Questions Féministes* collective.

Annie Leclerc has a degree in philosophy and taught philosophy until 1975. She has published novels and essays and has contributed to several journals, including *les Temps Modernes*.

Françoise Picq has been involved in the MLF since 1970, and with women's studies since 1975. She has participated in various theoretical, militant and research groups in the movement such as the *groupe d'études féministes* (feminist study group at the University of Paris 7). She was one of the organizers of the 1982 conference 'Femmes, féminisme et recherches': and she is a founder of the *Association pour les Etudes Féministes* in Paris. She has contributed many articles to journals and newspapers such as *le Torchon Brûle, la Revue d'en Face, les Temps Modernes* and *Pénélope*. She is a lecturer in political science at the University of Paris 9, and her research projects include feminism and socialism in the Third Republic, and a study of the MLF and its effects on French society.

Eliane Viennot has been involved in the MLF since 1974. She was active in the MLAC (movement for the freedom of abortion and contraception) and active in a far-left group *Révolution!* until 1977. She co-founded the feminist bookshop Carabosses in Paris where she worked until 1984. From 1978 to 1984 she was part of a group which worked on women in politics, writing a collective book *C'est terrible quand on y pense* (Galilée, 1982). She has also written many articles for feminist journals. Eliane Viennot took up her studies again two years ago and is currently writing her thesis on the relationship between women and politics in the sixteenth century. She is visiting scholar this year in the Department of Women's Studies at the University of Washington at Seattle.

Claire Duchen is a lecturer in French at Oxford Polytechnic.

Introduction to the collection

The women's liberation movement is international but has developed very differently in different countries. Debate and exchange is often a problem, not only because of language barriers and lack of translation – which, however, remain obstacles – but also because things don't always make sense when they are removed from their particular social, political and cultural context. I think that this is the case with the way that feminist texts from France have been received in Britain and elsewhere.

French feminists have the reputation of paying more attention to theory than to practical questions, and there is some truth in this: when a problem is discussed, more time is spent defining the terms of the debate and the nature of the problem than in looking for any practical solution. On the positive side, this means that intellectual debate is rigorous; but it also means that feminists in France have been slower than British feminists in 'networking', or in setting up rape crisis centres or refuges for battered women. Furthermore, feminist texts that are produced in France tend to find their way into English-speaking circles through French departments in universities and polytechnics, which are frequently literary, linguistic or philosophical in their focus. Both the texts that are likely to interest academic women and the kind of use made of them will exaggerate the tendency that we have to think of French feminism as highly theoretical and as having little in common with Anglo-Saxon feminism. Certain texts, certain writers, become known as representative of feminism in France, whereas the relation of the writers to the women's movement is often either ambiguous or very specific, and is not in the least representative of the thinking that is current within the movement. Such writers, including, for instance, Julia Kristéva, Hélène Cixous, Annie Leclerc and Luce Irigaray, have written fascinating, provocative and clearly important work in their exploration of women's relation to language, to the body, and to the unconscious. What remains absent from the way in which these texts are exported to other cultures is their original political context. Without the emergence of a struggle for women's liberation in France, as elsewhere, these texts would never have been written nor been read with the attention they now receive.

The first anthology of feminist writing from France in translation, *New French Feminisms*,[1]* was published in the USA in 1980 and, to my mind, perpetuates the image of a feminism that is preoccupied with questions of psychoanalysis and language to the exclusion of practically everything else. *French Connections* both complements that first anthology by redressing the balance, and also challenges it in the emphasis it seeks to maintain, portraying feminist thinking and activity in France in a way with which few feminists in France would identify. *French Connections* aims to introduce the French women's liberation movement (*mouvement de libération des femmes*, known as the MLF), and certain key debates within the movement to women who have not had access to these texts before. As the title reflects, I am convinced, perhaps optimistically, that there is more that connects British and French feminists than divides us: yet even where the issues and problems are the same in Britain and in France the debates have often taken a very different path in the two countries. This collection aims to explain aspects of feminist thinking in France that are unfamiliar, and also to shed a different light on questions that are well-known to women outside France. I hope that it will contribute to changing the image of French feminism from something that is interesting but largely irrelevant, to that of a sister movement that shares the concerns and the struggles of feminists everywhere.

French Connections has two sections, with introductions that set the articles and the theme under discussion in context.

The first section deals with the life of the MLF itself. The MLF has been more introspective and reflective about its own development than other movements and there is a substantial body of literature that has been written about the movement itself. To reflect this concern and to show certain approaches to thinking about the MLF, two articles (one from the

---

*Superior figures refer to the Notes and References at the end of each chapter.

radical feminist journal *Questions Féministes* (Feminist Issues), the other from *la Revue d'en Face*),[2] consider the MLF's first decade and its prospects for the future.

The second section takes four areas of feminist debate in France which have both theoretical and practical dimensions. The theoretical differences between different groups of the MLF have inevitably had practical consequences for the movement as a whole.

The first of these issues to be presented concerns the group *Psychanalyse et Politique* (*Psychoanalysis and Politics*, commonly called *Psych et Po*). This group may already be known to English-speaking feminists through the story that has been documented in French and in English[3] of how the group has registered the name and logo MLF as its own company title; how the now legal owners of the name 'women's liberation movement' profess their antifeminism;[4] how the wealth of one woman in the group allowed them to open bookshops, start a publishing company and finance a magazine, all with the name *des femmes* (some women/women/of women/by women/from women); how the group has initiated a number of court cases against authors, employees and against the feminist publisher Tierce.[5]

The intention of this anthology was to translate some texts from the *des femmes* magazine, so that women who had no knowledge of the group's ideas and style of writing would be given a taste of it: none of *Psych et Po*'s texts have been translated into English before. However, the editor and publishers regret that they have not been able to include this material because they were unable to reach agreement with the copyright holders for the permission necessary to reproduce the pieces. Women who would like to read *Psych et Po* texts for themselves should try to find the *des femmes* monthly and weekly magazines, and anything written by Antoinette Fouque.

This somewhat reduced section therefore contains only one article: an interview from *Le Matin* daily newspaper, between Catherine Clément and Antoinette Fouque.

The second issue in this section of the anthology is the question of women's 'difference' (one of *Psych et Po*'s major themes), which was also explored by women who were not connected with the group. Two texts represent opposing approaches to the question: the first, extracts from Annie Leclerc's book *Parole de Femme* (Woman's Word),[6] celebrates women's difference, women's bodies, 'woman-ness'. When it was published in

1974, it caused quite a stir, partly because Leclerc was the wife of the Marxist theoretician Nicos Poulantzas, and partly because this was the first time that a woman had spoken out so openly, personally and proudly about inhabiting a woman's body. Leclerc's book fuelled the debate over difference which has received more attention in France than it has in Britain. The second article on this issue argues fiercely against the position typified by Leclerc, and called the 'ideology of neo-femininity' by its author Colette Guillaumin. Guillaumin, originally a member of the *Questions Féministes* collective, argues that the question of women's difference must be discussed in its material, historical and political context. Once analysed in these terms, difference is exposed as synonymous with women's oppression, just as other differences (racial, class) have always been used to justify class oppression and racism.

The third issue is that of political lesbianism, also called radical lesbianism in France. This issue is always explosive and divisive, asking questions that will inevitably divide women who answer them differently. Can you be feminist and heterosexual? Is lesbianism a political position or a form of sexuality? Can it be both? Must it be both? Can men be political allies or are all men always the enemy? A split within the *Questions Féministes* collective in 1981 over political lesbianism brought the issue to the foreground in the MLF as a whole, with feelings and anger on both sides running high. Both sides of the initial split and of the wider debate are presented here.

A further group of texts deals with the issue of how feminists can, or – as seems more accurately to be the case – can't, make a political commitment that accounts for both their feminism and their affiliation to a political party. In the early days of the MLF, in the late 1960s and early 1970s, most feminists broke away from their party or their 'revolutionary' organization in the general denunciation of institutions. Many of them had been involved in ultra-left marginal groups – Maoist, Trotskyist, anarchist – that were influential during the events of May '68 but which subsequently lost all importance. However, as feminism gained currency in wider spheres, women within mainstream political parties began to feel the need to develop a feminist analysis from within the party and to challenge sexism in party ideology and structure and also in the behaviour of their party brothers. The texts translated here, from the feminist collective in the Communist Party (now no longer in the party), the feminist collective in the Socialist Party (mostly not in the party any more) and from a former member of a revolutionary organization, show the path that always seems to lead feminists to leave their party, unable to reconcile the two aspects of their political selves.

The anthology concludes with a long extract from an article called *Au Revoir*, first published in *les Cahiers du Grif* in 1978.[7] Françoise Collin, the author, meditates at length in this article about questions that affect and concern women's movements everywhere: success and its side-effects, sisterhood, reformism and co-option, strategies, long-term goals and the future. While she takes the French-speaking movement as her point of reference, her words will strike chords of recognition in many women. I think that Collin's article shows that, in spite of considerable cultural difference, women's liberation movements everywhere face the same dilemmas, ask the same questions, share the same aspirations, and need to learn from and with each other.

Notes and references

The translations are my own except where credit is given to another translator. Responsibility for accuracy and for all errors is mine alone.

1 First published by the University of Massachusetts Press in 1980 and in Britain by Harvester Press in 1982.
2 *la Revue d'en Face* is impossible to translate: it means to be at odds with something, to disagree. It also means to be opposite in the sense of facing someone or something. This journal, which ceased publication in 1983, was begun by a group of women with a variety of feminist political positions, some linked to mixed left-wing groups, others identifying as radical feminists.
3 In French, see *Chroniques d'une Imposture* (1981), a collection put together to describe the activities of *Psych et Po*. In English, see Jill Lewis in *Spare Rib*, no. 108 (1981), and my *Feminism in France* (Routledge and Kegan Paul, 1986).
4 *Psych et Po's* 'antifeminism' is based on the group's claim that feminism means power-seeking for women who want full integration into a male, masculine world. Feminism therefore denies women's difference and accepts the misogyny of patriarchy.
5 The *éditions des femmes*, which won the case, accused *Tierce* of *concurrence déloyale*, or 'unfair competition' in trading practices.
6 Published by Grasset (1974). *Parole* means word, voice, language, depending on the context. In the translation, I have used all three at different times.
7 *les cahiers du Grif* (Grif standing for Groupe de Recherche et d'Information Féministe – Feminist Research and Information Group) began in 1973,

the first French language feminist review to appear. Published by a group of women in Brussels, it had a wide readership in France as well. Each issue focuses on a particular theme (for instance, motherhood, women and politics, housework). The articles are annotated in the margins by other women, so that the reader has the impression of an ongoing debate. The *cahiers* had a four year break, from 1978 to 1982 and is now appearing again with a re-formed collective based in Paris and is published by *Tierce*.

PART ONE

The MLF: History and the Future

1 Introduction

How we as feminists can write our own history is a question that concerns women in France as elsewhere. We are all conscious of the difficulties of writing, and know that no single woman's experience, and no single 'version' of the history of the women's liberation movement can accurately represent the collective life of the movement.[1] But if we don't write our own history we allow our stories to be forgotten or, if written by someone else, possibly misrepresented.[2]

Françoise Picq, author of the first article in this section, felt that this was precisely what was happening in France in 1979–81. In her article, she responds to three events which, to different degrees, seemed either to tell the MLF story in a way which did not account for her own experience, or represented a public recasting of what the MLF was and what it had achieved – by *Psych et Po* on the one hand, and by the new (1981) Socialist government on the other.

In 1981, a book by Naty Garcia Guadilla, a sociologist and active feminist, was published: *Libération des Femmes, le MLF*,[3] (Women's Liberation, the MLF). Guadilla's book told the story of the MLF from 1968 to 1979 in a way that was widely felt to oversimplify the reality of the movement. Picq, while acknowledging Guadilla's book as a valuable contribution to feminist history, was concerned that her own experience within the movement was not represented in the book. Guadilla's history presents the MLF as a movement divided into three 'currents': three different types of feminism, operating independently, each having its own approach to women's oppression and women's liberation. *Psych et Po* was one of these, with its emphasis on psychoanalytic theory as a way to the recovery of repressed 'woman-ness', or 'femininity', from the unconscious; the second current was the *tendance lutte des classes* (class struggle current), which saw feminism as a more or less integral part of the struggle for socialism, and involved women who gave priority to the exploration of the relationship between feminism and socialism, either from a position of feminist autonomy or from inside a mixed political organization as well. The third current grew out of the small active group *Féministes Révolutionnaires*[4] and became identified mainly as radical feminism.

These three currents did indeed exist. But, Picq argues, the early days of the MLF must not be forgotten and swamped because of the way the movement developed later. In 1970–2 or so the movement was able to absorb a variety of approaches to the question of what women's oppression actually was and how women should fight it. The currents hadn't always existed, nor did they develop at the same time nor last for the same length of time, nor did any one current dominate the collective life of the MLF. Picq reminds us that women who identified as feminists didn't necessarily see themselves as part of one current or another, and she points to her own involvement which spanned different currents. Most women no doubt agreed with different currents on different issues and many may have felt no affinity with any of them. The MLF's reality was far less clear cut than Guadilla's book suggests and the boundaries between different approaches to feminism were not always rigidly maintained.

Picq, as well as Christine Delphy, author of the second article, also responds to the implications of *Psych et Po*'s legal ownership of the name MLF, which had taken the movement totally by surprise, and was discovered only by accident when a woman read of the registration of the name in 1979. There had been conflicts of several kinds between *Psych et Po* and other groups in the MLF since the mid 1970s, over its theory, its group dynamic, its relationship to the rest of the movement, its public statements and its antifeminism.[5] There were attempts to organize events together such as the 6 October 1979 march against the possible repeal of the abortion law, but each time there were problems, and other women gradually decided that it was impossible to work with *Psych et Po*. When it was discovered that the group had registered the name MLF as a commercial company title, even those feminists who had previously extended goodwill were understandably alarmed and angry. It was feared that as the 'official' MLF, *Psych et Po* would manage to impose its own views as the MLF 'line' on questions, when there was never actually one MLF line on anything. It was feared that *Psych et Po* would gain public credibility as feminists while putting forward the group's own very specific, rather exclusive version of what the MLF was. This has not in fact happened to date, but at the beginning of the decade, the threat seemed very serious and potentially damaging for the future of the movement.

Delphy's article shows how past, present and future are linked, and how, from the *Psych et Po* lesson, feminists should learn that the writing of history is vital. She rejects the commonly held idea that history is an objective narrative, telling the story of 'what really happened', but she claims it as a terrain for feminist struggle, as a political act.

As the fear of co-option by *Psych et Po* faded, it was replaced by fears of a different kind. In 1981, the left came to power for the first time in twenty-five years, with a Socialist President and a majority of Socialists in parliament. At first this created a huge wave of excitement among feminists, who hoped for new initiatives from the government concerning women, and who also hoped that feminism as a means of political analysis would be considered with a new seriousness by those in power. The years of the Socialist period in office proved to be a disappointment in some ways, and even its successes have their limitations.

One major achievement, for instance, was the foundation of a Ministry for Women's Rights, with a small budget but a budget nevertheless.[6] Its efforts were mostly aimed at changing legislation and practices concerning women at work, women's health care and so on. The Minister, Yvette Roudy, acknowledged that 'mentalities' lag behind legislation and such changes that are made in law can always disappear. There is a clear need for a body such as the Ministry, and Roudy and her advisers fought for women within the terms of their mandate. However, the existence of the Ministry had several effects on the women's movement. First, a more 'official' feminism came to the foreground, marginalizing others more than ever; second, it is hard to disagree with the efforts made by this institutionalized feminism, for criticism can be used against feminism in general rather than against a particular approach or against the limitations of the institution; third, the Socialists in government and the existence of a Ministry for Women's Rights changed the relationship of the MLF to power, brought the question of reform and co-option into play and, in my view, contributed to a real change of feminist political identity. In her 1981 article, Picq argues for renewed attention to structure and calls for the MLF to adapt in the light of changes – both changes inside the movement and changes in French political life generally; both Picq and Delphy ask questions concerning the relation of the MLF to the 'outside' and to institutions; both articles consider the MLF's past and its prospects for the future at a moment of pivotal significance. Picq's article ranges over the decade of 1971–81, looking at specific events and developments within the MLF, while Delphy's moves from the specifics of the MLF's history, opening out on to questions that are at first anchored in the French women's movement but that can later be used as a point of comparison with the experience of others.

With the return of the right to power in March 1986, the Ministry for Women's Rights has been abolished. The 1986 elections have indeed revealed the fragility of 'institutionalized feminism', and have made women aware that the relationship of feminism to the state must be constantly reassessed.

Notes and references

1   There are at the moment collective projects under way in France, (including some sponsored by the state research institute, the CNRS) to put together a history of the MLF.

2   At this point, I have to say that my own writing of a history of the MLF has caused me many moments of anxiety at the thought that I might be misrepresenting women's experience. I think that the only way round this is to remain sensitive to the variety of experience but also to make no claims to be representative.

3   Published by PUF in 1981.

4   The term 'revolutionary feminists' is different in meaning in France and in Britain. This group in France consisted of women who would probably call themselves radical feminists today, with many differing ideas about women's oppression and how to fight it. The group splintered into many small collectives, grouped around specific projects and joining together on an *ad hoc* basis to organize larger events and conferences.

5   *Psych et Po* and the group leader Antoinette Fouque have always stated their opposition to all 'isms' (see Fouque's interview with Catherine Clément, pp. 50–4).

6   Under the Presidency of Valéry Giscard d'Estaing, there was a Secretariat on the Condition of Women, which had no independent budget at all and which was therefore completely powerless. Its goal had been to 'make recommendations concerning women to the Prime Minister's office'.

2 The MLF: run for your life*

Françoise Picq

Over the ten years or so since the MLF began, many things have changed, and we haven't really weighed up the extent of the changes. And the women's movement isn't what it used to be, even though it sticks to its old anti-organizational principles. Ten years on seems to be a good time to pause and reflect on what has happened so far. These appraisals are appearing all over the place – autobiographies, theses, essays, different kinds of studies – and in all of them, I can at best only recognize a small part of my own experience in the movement. Mostly these accounts make me feel as though I've been betrayed.

For some time now I have felt a real need to leave a record of what the MLF was, to draw up a sort of balance-sheet, to tell the story so far and see what the MLF has become since the early days. I have participated in many collective attempts to tell our story, all of which have failed, but that doesn't mean we don't need to do it. We do, more so now than ever before. There is a certain degree of nostalgia in my desire to leave traces of our history. The movement no longer belongs to the women who were there at the beginning: it somehow escapes our desires and our conflicts. It has its own life, which isn't necessarily the same as ours, but I feel that I am one of those responsible for it. My fear of our disappearing is also linked to our discovery of the history of feminism which had been so misrepresented for so long. But it is also that, today, in the hope that the new political situation may open up new possibilities, it seems urgent to take stock of the situation and to think about the ideas and concepts we use, how ever clumsily we manage.

Reading Naty Garcia's book *Libération des Femmes, le MLF* has made me react quite strongly. She has accomplished an enormous amount and I

*Edited, shortened version, from *La Revue d'en Face*, no. 11. 1981.

have learned a lot of things from her. But I can't accept her version of the early days of the movement, which she describes as being in rigid currents – I can't locate my own experience in any one current and I am not the only one who feels this. At the beginning, there was a great deal of flexibility and everyone participated in her own way in the collective events (*Manifesto of the 343*, the 20 November march, meetings at the Mutualité);[1] it didn't matter who initiated and organized them. While certain currents were dominant here or there, none of the groups was exclusive. For instance, I was never involved with any of the groups started by the *Feministes Révolutionnaires*, but I *did* do certain things with them, such as produce one issue of the newspaper *Le Torchon Brûle*:[2] I never felt part of the 'class struggle current' although I was active in a mixed political group, but I *did* participate in local women's groups;[3] I went to *Psychanalyse et Politique* meetings although I didn't agree with the group, and I broke definitively with them in 1972–3. The problems I've had and still have with each of these currents have never made me feel like an outsider, which means that I can state with conviction that the movement was something more than the sum of three currents. We must be careful not to project back to the beginning of the movement situations that only developed later on. What we must rather do is evaluate what the movement has become in the light of the richness of the beginning and the hopes we had invested in it.

It is no accident that the MLF grew out of the turmoil of May '68 – or rather, in its aftermath. It shared May '68's overwhelming desire to change the world, to liberate speech; it shared in the massive political awareness that was developing outside traditional political structures. But the MLF only really appeared after the May Movement, with its small militant and sectarian group structure, as women realized that their hopes would not be fulfilled in the May Movement and that the anti-hierarchy discourse of the men was contradicted by their political practice. Women realized that far-left groups perpetuated women's oppression through the power struggles inside the groups, the way that men monopolized discussions, spoke in a masculine political language with which women did not identify, the way that the sexual division of political activity was maintained, and the way that women were, in general, kept in inferior positions.

The MLF's affiliation to, and then reaction to, the May Movement, explains its character as a political movement, and also its choice of spontaneity, shock tactics and alternative practices. As heir(ess) to May '68, it also reacted against the formal procedures of far-left groups, and proclaimed that women would not seek power or have leaders. The MLF rejected structuring its debates, with lists of speakers, someone in the chair, majority decisions, etc. In contrast to masculine discourse, based on knowledge and power, the MLF paid great attention to the subjective, to pooling personal experiences. In contrast to the notion that the more militant you are, the more 'saved' you'll be, to the idea that the activist is superior, understands the oppression suffered by the oppressed, and speaks on their behalf, we invented a new political practice, with each woman speaking about herself, about ourselves and in our own names only.

The MLF's great originality was to insist on being a women-only movement. To meet in women-only groups in the early 1970s was scandalous, was ridiculed and was a problem for many women who thought it was a step backwards, back to girls' schools and to the time when women were excluded from social life.

The violence of men's reactions to this women-only principle helped us judge its importance. A women-only principle was forbidden in the name of the revolution – which men alone controlled – and seeing that men wanted to control us as well, we also saw that we had to gain our individual and collective autonomy. Together we found that everything was changing, that we dared to speak out and that what we had to say and the way we said it wasn't the same any more – we didn't keep to men's norms or use the same points of reference.

We found that the trappings of power had gone: there were no leaders versus rank-and-file, but only women, superb and each one different, to be discovered and loved. We all listened to each other, met new women, experienced solidarity between women and discovered a new way of being ourselves and of being politically active.

The women-only nature of the MLF was here to stay and was difficult to explain to outsiders. We were always questioned and criticized about this by new women, and all we could do was welcome them and wait for them to see why it was a women-only movement – which never took long.

When Naty describes the movement as divided into two currents from the very beginning, I have to protest all the more vigorously because I tried to stop the two currents from forming. There were always different opinions in the movement – feminist, Marxist, homo – or hetero – each one had its own way of doing things, its own approach, its own past and its own ideas. It is easy to assume that the currents that came into being later in the

MLF's existence were the same thing as the early disagreements, but that would be to rewrite the MLF's history wrongly, obscuring its richness. If these currents had always existed, the MLF would have evolved differently; as it was, the movement provided the space for many different approaches to join together with the same hopes and desires. Small groups formed here and there, as friendships developed, meeting to discuss various topics: jealousy, violence, sexuality – and then everyone joined together for regular open meetings and for collective events. It was the beginning of a kind of unorganized organization.

Gradually, however, differences became more pronounced; there was a loss of confidence and things didn't go well between the various groups. However, there were women in each current who rejected the idea that antagonistic clans were forming, and we formed the 'Thursday group'. After a women's demonstration against the Vietnam war, a group met to discuss the event. We wanted to think about our practice without being paralysed by an established critical perspective, without accepting either the 'act first think later' approach of some women, or the *Psych et Po* theory-substitute-for-action. We wanted to think about our relationship to institutions – to work, to the universities we were involved in; to find a path between integration on the one hand, and the female ghetto on the other. We wanted to discover our relationship *as women* to what was going on, to politics outside the MLF.

According to Naty, the theoretical divergences between *Psych et Po* and the *Féministes Révolutionnaires* was 'clearly caused by the fact that the latter accepted that they were in the same lineage as feminists from the nineteenth and early twentieth centuries'. In fact, the *Féministes Révolutionnaires*' claim was far more abstract: 'it means we are for women, before anything else', giving priority to allegiance to sex over allegiance to class, they weren't really interested in the past. It was only much later that we wanted to uncover our heritage and that we were able to find the same preoccupations, the same contradictions, the same analyses in early feminism as we had.

Many issues divided feminists at the beginning of the century, preventing them from joining together, but the issues they raised concern and inform us all. The struggle that these women engaged in has taught me not to assume that individual ambition and collective struggle are in opposition; these 'firsts' – at university, in the professions, forcing open doors that were previously closed to women – fought 'not only for themselves but for all women'. I have learned that feminism couldn't exist without women's ambition – individual and collective – and that it is this that drives us forwards.

The MLF invented a new kind of politics based on our own lives, in order to change them. There were the occasional attempts at 'entryism', in department stores or women's workshops, attempts to get talking to women in markets or in other local open spaces like playgrounds or squares, but on the whole the women's movement fed off itself, found enough inside itself to keep it going. We despised everyone who wasn't part of the MLF – reformist groups, the Family Planning Association. We had the nerve to believe that we had invented a radically new and unique type of thought. At first, this wasn't really a problem, because the MLF was constantly changing, coming up with new ideas and structures, and it had repercussions outside, in other groups – possibly less radical but certainly more active, so that, 'co-opted' or not, MLF ideas found a place within the institution. But a time came when the MLF, a Parisian, intellectual, narcissistic group, became a ghetto.

We had rejected far-left political practice but we hadn't found anything with which to replace it. Aware of our own cultural and professional privileges, we still hoped that other women would join us, that they would be like us and that we didn't need to go and actively seek them out or talk down to them. We had started the MLF as a reaction to global, all-encompassing ideologies and perspectives – but we were overwhelmed by feelings of defeat, impotence, uselessness.

Consciously or nor, we had a 'co-option strategy'. In other words, we had the ideas, took up radical postures, and allowed those who worked inside institutions to turn our ideas into reforms. And then we would protest at the way our struggle was being deformed by the institutions – and keep our integrity intact.

It worked quite well with the abortion issue – although the government didn't respond to our demand for the abolition of the 1920 law[4] and allowed abortion only with very unsatisfactory conditions attached to the new law. It was, however, a law that we didn't dare oppose. Our fight against rape showed up the danger of our strategy more clearly. We wanted rape to be recognized as a criminal act. Taking us at our word, the judiciary decided that rapists were indeed criminals, had to be punished and locked up, and they refused to listen to what women had to say about it. No doubt judges now recognize that when women say no they mean no, and that they are not always guilty of provoking male lust; but it is never acknowledged that rape is anything other than individual deviant behaviour by naughty lambs who must be kept away from the flock. We felt uneasy in the repressive role of the injured party in a court case. By becoming involved in the wheels of justice, we lost control over what we were doing – and there we were, protestors against the system, now turned into hostages of repressive 'security and freedom' policies,[5] hostages of social control.

The new (1981) situation, still unsettled, no doubt opens up new perspectives. We could, of course, continue our 'co-option' strategy, hoping that the new government, whose ideas are closer to our own, will not deform what we have to say as much as the last government. It's tempting – it is the easy thing to do; it avoids disagreement among ourselves, and it keeps our hands clean in our common inability to do anything. I personally feel that this position would be a refusal to take a historic opportunity; if we now have the chance to act, to influence the way that society evolves, to influence legislation and improve the material conditions of women's lives, then we must take on our responsibilities. We can't just let the new government use us: we must initiate actions and see them through. However, if we are going to make this kind of strategic change, it clearly means that we also have to make far-reaching transformations in the women's movement as it is today.

We often feel that 'young women' aren't coming to the movement to ensure the continued existence of the MLF and we try to find out why they are so hesitant. But when you think about it, the women who founded the MLF in 1970, or came to it soon afterwards, weren't teenagers, although the media portrayed us as kids. We all had a political history, a political past: May '68, alternative left politics, communal living. In our personal lives too, we had had our share of difficulties and disappointments: failures, break-ups, abortions, rapes. Our revolt stemmed precisely from these experiences and we weren't surprised that, apart from coming to demonstrations, very young women weren't attracted to the movement. But the movement itself was young and that is what gave it its youthful image. This wonderment at a sort of birth, recognition of ourselves and each other, gave us the extraordinary feeling that we were starting everything anew. What we wrote then seems naïve today, but we haven't been so creative, so imaginative, and fruitful since then. The movement has grown up.

I want to stress this question of age, because I'm convinced that the movement's current difficulties are a kind of difficulty in growing up, in finding an adult identity. Maybe we are concerned about the lack of young women coming to the movement because we don't want our movement to grow old – but this is not only an illusion, it is also dangerous.

We may not have changed our positions, but we haven't got the same energy to put them into practice as we used to; all the more so since we now frequently find ourselves in established roles – mother, mother-in-law, aunt, teacher – facing young people who see our principles as a traditional kind of moralism. If the movement really is growing old without being renewed by a new generation, maybe it's time for us to come to terms with this, so that it matures as we do and doesn't dry up.

We weren't 18 in 1970 – we're not 20 now! Most of us don't have the same lifestyle that we had then; as students with no responsibilities, the movement took up all our time, we were carried along by it. Now our lives have separated us more from each other – in our jobs, our relationships, our children. We have made compromises in our lives, carving out our own niches for ourselves. We have also had disappointments in the movement; there have been many personal quarrels. Sisterhood has often been dramatically shown up to be a lie.

And while young women aren't coming to the MLF, the older ones are leaving; the movement can't accommodate their changed lives. Not only is it a women-only movement, but it excludes children. It was understandable that we didn't think about motherhood then – it wasn't our problem. Our problem was in fact to construct a new female identity not prescribed by motherhood. This must have kept out many women who hadn't made the same radical choices about their lives as we had.

But what about now? Ten years on? How many women have been trying to reconcile two clashing sides of their lives – or trying to choose between them?

I'm sure that many women who aren't involved any more cherish the memory of a women-only atmosphere, especially if their daily lives are heavily involved with men and children. But its hard to be involved in the MLF without being *totally* involved: the movement is exclusive and centrifugal – its excludes those who aren't available, simply by lack of information. Its informal power system depends on contact networks. How can you know what's going on when you aren't there? There aren't any newsletters, no formal communication; the movement is elusive, escapes us and must be understood from the centre because there isn't an outer edge. We have been talking recently about setting up a federation of MLF groups,[6] but who knows what the MLF is today? Who knows all the different groups? I don't, for a start. If we want a federation of our groups that won't end with one group taking over, we have to start by keeping all of us informed: we have to keep track of our groups, find out about them and what they're doing, get to know each other, confront each other's ideas; we have to keep track of projects and disagreements. We must publish a sort of catalogue of our resources. We can't work together unless there is a formal way of circulating information. We also need this so that the movement can welcome women who have less time and who are confused by the lack of structure and by the specific rather elitist character of the MLF.

The spontaneity that we had in the beginning was wonderful but also had its problems: the movement can't want to be eternally young anymore than it can confer eternal youth on us. And in the same way that we all have to find our own adult identity, the movement has to come to roost, put some roots down somewhere.

Whatever happened to our principles? What has our confidence and our naïvety led us to? Obviously our rejection of organization, our glorification of spontaneity and subjectivity has freed women's voices and women's actions; and obviously our confidence has allowed us to discover ourselves, and working together has helped us liberate our energies. But look at what we've got now! The MLF's lack of formality has allowed invisible and therefore all the more dangerous power to settle in. Our ideological struggle has become a struggle between sisters; rather than helping us to move forward through the dynamic of contradiction, the lack of formality has paralysed the movement, has turned it into a closed world in which rival factions confront each other.

In our reaction to the way that male-dominated groups operated, we thought that we had created a space where no one thing was right and everything else was wrong. We thought that 'power', a masculine phenomenon, didn't concern us, and that we were sisters, equal and different. But we let in another kind of power: seduction by impressive speakers, fascination by one woman's words to the point that everyone would imitate her. Because we didn't believe in rivalry and we put our ideas together, we lost the identity of individual women's contributions (as texts were written unsigned), which later allowed other women to claim them as their own.

Nobody could speak in the name of all women, nobody could sign something on behalf of the whole MLF – and suddenly one group claims to be the legal owner of the MLF and refuses to let all other women say that they are part of it. Because we didn't delegate responsibilities and power, we denied ourselves any control over this informal, but none the less very real, power, and in order to keep to our principles, we condemned ourselves to inaction.

Psych et Po is only the caricature of a phenomenon which exists inside the MLF; it is dangerous not only because it claims to *be* the MLF while speaking against it from outside, but also because it uses up our energies in fighting it and betrays the hopes we placed in the MLF, in its spontaneity; it divides us and makes us all suspicious of each other. Today, any initiative or action taken is suspected of being power-seeking, and our inability to act is one of the MLF's less divisive aspects.

To save our potential for the future, we have no choice but to rethink, radically, all the notions we were so sure of at the beginning. We have to look to the great democratic principles founded by men in order to keep tyranny at bay. We can't be confident that women can bypass democratic formality, which is the only way to guarantee our liberty, our equality: it must be organized. There is obviously no question of fitting the MLF into a mould set up by someone else. But to perpetuate structurelessness is the sure way to help *Psych et Po* rob us of ourselves and to keep the movement prey to unspoken anti-democratic power, different levels of availability, secret networks of women.

If, in our diverse and separate lives, we feel the need for the women's movement to continue, if we also believe in the need for a space where an autonomous, women-only, feminist theory or feminist project can develop, we have to learn to live together and take our difficulties and contradictions into account. By trusting each other and remaining alert (but not suspicious), we have to learn tolerance and mutual respect. We have to set up structures where collective decisions can be taken, without a power struggle, without manipulation and with respect for minority positions. Why shouldn't women be capable of this? After ten years of the MLF, has all our energy and confidence been sapped?

We no longer believe in this universal women's sisterhood that is self-evident and doesn't need to be watched, but we still have a significant and lucid critique of what we rejected in masculine organizations and what we have to change in the women's movement.

And I, personally, believe that in the political climate which began in May 1981 there is surely a place for a women's movement.

Notes and references

1   The Mutualité is a large hall in Paris where many big political meetings take place.

2   *Le Torchon Brûle* (The Burning Rag/Dishcloth) was the first feminist newspaper to appear in 1970. It was run collectively and each issue (there were only seven in all, including the first issue which was a special supplement to an anarchist newspaper) was produced by a different group of women. Its goal was to express all the different ideas and experiences of women in the MLF, share news and publicize events.

3   The local women's groups were mostly organized by women who identified with the 'class struggle tendency'.

4   The 1920 law prohibited abortion and contraception and allowed for prosecution of all those who aborted, helped a woman procure an abortion, performed an abortion, provided information about contraception and provided contraceptive material. Contraception was legalized in France in 1967, and abortion, with constraints and conditions, in 1975.

5   'Security and freedom' was the name of a repressive law initiated by the Giscardian Minister of Justice, Alain Peyrefitte.

6   After the election of the left in 1981, many feminists wanted to set up a federation of feminist groups that would speak for the MLF while representing all the different MLF groups. The idea foundered at its first meeting, held at the Mutualité on 9 June 1981. Françoise Picq was among the women who had the initial idea for the federation and argued persuasively in favour of it.

3 Women's liberation: the tenth year*

Christine Delphy

Ten years after the emergence of the women's liberation movement (MLF), there are still people like Georges Marchais[1] who talk about 'the liberation of Woman', forgetting the plural that makes all the difference between a myth and beings of flesh and blood. Still, although only a few people can spell it right, no one can ignore the movement any more. The journalist who, boasting about his home region, writes with patriarchal fatuousness, 'where I live, we've never heard of the MLF' shows simply by writing these words that this movement he hasn't heard of is still useful to him, in however negative a way, in order to define the region he comes from. When sexism is mentioned, eight times out of ten it is to deny that it has any importance or that it exists at all, but the notion itself does exist, where there hadn't even been a word for it before. The road we've covered can be measured by the distance between the 'I'm not a feminist but' of pre-1970, and the 'I'm not a sexist but' of 1980. The 'non-sexist' may still follow his 'but' with 'You just have to look to see that women's hands are better adapted than men's to wringing out floor cloths'; the feminist vision of the world may constantly be challenged, it doesn't matter – what matters is that it is taken into account.

This is so obvious, so ordinary, that we tend to forget that it hasn't always been like this, and that at least 'at the level of discourse', we've changed our world, we've changed the world. And this other world, where nobody needed to challenge feminism because it didn't exist, where men didn't have to defend themselves for being something that no one dreamed of accusing them of being, is not so long ago: it is only ten years ago. Even those women who were responsible for this change haven't always realized

*From *Questions Féministes*, no. 7, 1980.

the enormity of it, and sometimes forget that, before, they couldn't even imagine it.

It is a pity: because if we take for granted a situation that we created ourselves, then what will those women who have never known the pre-MLF world make of it? If, forgetting where our present society comes from, we underestimate the distance we have made society travel, it doesn't matter for us, but it does for the women who follow us. How will they know what our society would have been like without our struggles? Yes, it could be – it has been – worse than it is today. Who will tell them that our struggles and our struggles alone made things change, and it is only their struggles that will take them further? How will they defend themselves against the dominant ideology which, always, in its many different forms, presents the few centimetres snatched from our oppressors through our struggle as the result of 'progress-which-just-happens', a semi-natural process, like continents shifting?

If I am talking in this article about the 'cultural' achievements of the movement (the 'level of discourse') it is not because I want to ignore or undervalue concrete achievements: the staggering extension of the movement, the proliferation of groups, projects and actions; the uncovering, exposing and denunciation of enormous areas of oppression; the organization of huge campaigns and victories – incomplete, no doubt, but victories all the same – against the most immediate, the most physical violence, such as enforced childbearing and enforced sexual intercourse. If I speak here about cultural achievements, it is because they can be real anchor points, from which the general level of consciousness can be raised – or not raised. If the dominant ideology wins, these achievements can be lost as soon as they are won. If the liberalizing of abortion laws results from the 'inevitable evolution of society' and if women's liberation is the 'unavoidable consequence' of 'more democracy', then our struggles have been for nothing – they will tell later generations that it would all have happened anyway.

And the dominant ideology doesn't only deny the usefulness of our past struggles by attributing all the recent changes to the system, it confers on the system the (semblance of) ability to change by itself. And if the system changes by itself, then struggling at all is as stupid as running upstairs next to an escalator: it wears you out for nothing, you end up in the same place. So our past and present struggles can be used against future struggles, they can be of more use to the system than no struggles at all, if the system manages to create an image of intrinsic mobility by stealing our own achievements from us, if we allow it to take possession of them and parade them as its own.

There are already 18-year-old women who do not understand the founding principles of a movement which is barely ten years old: they neither understand why the principles were necessary nor what a huge step was made in actually putting our principles into practice. For instance, the principle of women-only meetings: 'but', they say, 'our men are really quite nice, they're not sexist'. It is not enough to shake our grey heads and chuckle into our (old) beards. When they say that their lives are not – not exactly anyway – what ours were at their age, they are right. The tragedy is that the changes – whatever they are and whether they are thought of as big or small – are being used as arguments against the struggle.

How could such a thing have happened? Ten years on, it is time to stop and think, to try and understand not only this but other things as well. Time to see where we are, how we got here and where we can go from here. 1980 will be the year of drawing things together, of taking stock of the situation, of assessment. We have accumulated experiences: we now have to bring them together, analyse them and make use of them, collectively. There are so many topics for us to think about that it would be impossible even to begin to enumerate them, and anyway they must be established collectively. However it would not be fair to approach this assessment of the movement in an exaggeratedly self-critical spirit; 1980 should also be a year for celebration! For many of the problems we are now experiencing are due to the very success of the movement.

In fact, the two kinds of problems that are mentioned the most frequently (and just as much in other countries as in France) result, in the last instance, from the diffusion of feminist ideas, on the one hand, and from the structure of the movement itself on the other, from its way of operating, which is also one of its successes. The first kind of problem – difficulty of co-ordinating and even of simply circulating information within the movement – is undoubtedly linked to the horizontal way the movement spreads, like cells dividing, and to the way that the groups function autonomously, which is itself good, and positive. The second kind of problem revolves around the difficulty, which also seems to be increasing, of making the movement's voice, or rather the voice of radicalism, be heard and singled out, when it is mixed into a chorus of voices, louder and louder, more and more generalized, talking about women.

The frustration that this state of affairs causes can provoke an antagonistic reaction to everything that 'is not part of the movement' (we don't always know what the movement is, but we always know what it isn't), an anger which also confuses reformism and co-option. Whereas it is very important to distinguish between the two and also to analyse this instant hostility towards everything 'that isn't us'.

While we rejoice when feminism reaches a sister, a mother, a friend, we paradoxically condemn the collective expression of this moment of consciousness-raising. How many times have we heard the words 'watering down', 'betrayal' or even 'co-option' used to talk about timid feminist positions. What is happening there is that we're showing a lack of awareness of the consciousness-raising process, which we've been through ourselves and should know about. It also shows our lack of understanding of how ideas are spread as well as an unrealistic and politically suspect desire to keep control over the ideas we launch. Not everything that uses feminist ideas, with or without quotation marks, is co-option: to say that is to deny other women, women who are not part of us, the right to express themselves, it is to condemn ourselves to an isolation that is luckily impossible because it is to want an empty space between revolutionaries and conservatives, which would be dangerous if it were conceivable; it is to deny the inevitable and necessary role of reformism. Co-option most certainly exists; it is dangerous, and to confuse it with reformism is to deprive ourselves of the means to fight it effectively. Co-option begins *not* when feminist ideas or expressions are used, but when they are turned inside out, when they are used against the movement's goals or against the movement itself. These problems are linked to the way the movement has developed historically and we must work together to examine how they have arisen. But history, here, is not just a context, as it is for everything that happens through time. History is implicated in a more direct way, especially in the question of co-option; for it is by the constant re-writing of history, by the theft of our achievements, that our future is threatened.

We try to learn from the history of other oppressed groups and from the history of the first feminist movement. Through our struggles we found out that the history of women's struggles, fighting for their own interests, is not important for purely or even primarily academic reasons; and that the suppression and distortion of these struggles by 'official' history is not an academic question either. It is hardly accidental that so much feminist energy throughout the world is now devoted to rediscovering the feminist struggles of the nineteenth and twentieth centuries. These struggles were buried, but not completely – or rather not just buried. Patriarchy is too subtle simply to settle for erasing feminists from history: in patriarchal history, feminists survive, but look at the state of them! It is worse than if they hadn't been mentioned at all. They survive, hanging from the gallows of their books, exposed to all as a horrible lesson of what you mustn't do if you don't want to end up like them; corpses desecrated as an example to us all.

It was not enough to suppress their analyses, to deform their words – by omission as well as by actions – to smear their characters, to disfigure their ideals; they also had to present feminist undertakings not only as ridiculous and useless (since progress marches on by itself), but also as divisive (of the working class, of national unity, of family harmony, of dogs and cats, of women themselves) and also as pernicious because, in the last instance, it goes against its own goals – women's liberation, which, as we know, is achieved by cajoling the oppressors, not by getting on their nerves. It was not enough to kill our sisters a second time, in print; it was not enough to make us orphans of our own history. They also had to make us deny solidarity with our sisters, to make us reject them, using our enemies' words; they still were not satisfied with making us think that our sisters had actually been our enemies, nor with making us collaborate in their post-humous degradation, they also made us preface any protest against our oppression, however timid it may be, by cancelling out that protest in advance, forcing us to annul our denunciations by, in the same breath, swearing allegiance to patriarchy and renouncing any idea of revolt; they had to plunge us – and plunge we did – into the supreme abjectness (and those who were over 20 in 1970 will know what I mean) of saying '*I'm not a feminist* but. . . .'

If we now understand the importance of history, if we are weighing up today the ravages caused by patriarchy's annihilation and distortion of our history, will we finally understand the importance of the present, of what is happening in the movement today? This history – ours – is already written. And mainly by other people. And how it's being written! We are too ready to consider that history is the business of academics and we, on the other hand, are activists (even though there are now several projects to write the movement's history that have been around for two years or so). We seem to think that it's normal that people outside the movement write our history; and also normal that, being 'outside', they write it 'badly'. And that the distortions of our present history are just one facet of co-option, just as inevitable, and also not really dangerous in the long term. For a start, it doesn't stop us from doing things, and action is the most important thing of all: because they may write history, but we – we are *making* it.

When we think like this, we are implying that history is simply an account or description of reality, a description which, whether good or bad, faithful or not, nevertheless does not modify its 'subject' – that is, reality. Thinking like this is thinking that there is a level, other than the account itself, where the facts are written; a reality of the past. While it may seem obvious, this way of lookings at things is nothing less than an illusion. 'In reality', history does not exist outside the written account. And whoever writes history is making history. But, it will be argued, if we talk about the way we changed the abortion law, no one can say that we didn't because the law is well and truly changed. No, no one can say that the law isn't changed. Through our campaigns and our practices we forced the politicians to change the law: the fact that the law has changed remains true. But the fact that the government was forced into it? And forced by us? 'But everybody knows that.'

Who is 'everybody'? For readers of *Le Figaro*[2] it is Madame Veil[3] who has changed the law; for readers of *L'Humanité*,[4] it is 'the pressures brought by democratic parties'. Even among us, not everybody knows that the women's liberation movement and it alone was responsible for the abortion campaign. In 1976, in a local women's group I saw a chronology of the struggle for legal abortion in which it was said that the struggle began in 1972 and began with the manifesto of the doctors.[5] Where was the women-only women's movement in all this? It was not there, only five years afterwards; it had been wiped out of its own history by a feminist group. And what lesson could we learn for the future, what lesson could women, arriving in that group for the first time, learn from history as it was written in that simple chronology? If the abortion campaign came out of a *mixed* and *not* especially feminist organization, why should other campaigns for women's liberation not be run along the same lines? Where was the need for a feminist movement?

What is happening – not only in collectives working on abortion but also in 'autonomous' groups and elsewhere – for young women who call themselves feminists to be questioning our women-only principle, or even the principle of a women's movement? It is clear that in one way or another, for lack of attention, lack of interest or lack of the means to do it, we have not succeeded in really transmitting our experience to them. Our victories in the areas we call 'real' are not actually real, not really *won* if we allow the system – and the system is everywhere – to keep the results and take the movement's role away. This is what has already happened, or rather is still happening, insidiously and tirelessly.

Asking ourselves the question 'Where can we go from here?' implies that we ask how, in what conditions, our achievements can be used as a basis for new struggles. And for them to do so we must first and foremost assert and reassert the very idea of the struggle, the need for it, and its effectiveness; the struggle against the all-encompassing system, which spends its time keeping score and hiding the real protagonists and denying the process that has produced the winning score, that is, struggle. And we must write all the different moments of the struggle and especially the most important of them – the process of collective reflection through which we arrived at the positions that we later defended – into history.

We have the rather sad advantage over other oppressed groups of knowing (because we still have in front of us the fifty years during which feminism disappeared between 1920 and 1970) that our movements are mortal. We also know what efficient weapons the assaults by our enemy on our history have been; we have been able to measure the extent to which the patriarchal operation 'history', by depriving us of any tradition, any legitimacy, any achievements, has kept back and then disadvantaged the renaissance of a movement which had to reinvent everything, even its first idea that 'we are right to rebel'.[6] If the manipulation of history and the existence of a movement in reality are so linked, as history shows us, then we have to conclude that history is more than a narrative, it is a political stake. It is time that we realized that our history – that is, a narrative that unfolds from day to day, every day, of what happens every day – is something else, something more than simple representation – right or wrong but not affecting the thing represented – of struggles which only ever take place on other terrain. It is time we realized that history is part of reality, that it is itself an area of struggle.

In fact, whether we know it or not, it is already a battlefield. The system that twists our history, keeping the laws and throwing out the feminists, this system of selective record-keeping, is not only or even mainly located in the major institutions where we like to think that power resides. It is everywhere where things are said or written. And this system isn't just set in motion at certain times: history is made and unmade every day. It is every day that the movement is despoiled and attacked, because the two inevitably go together.

In order to discredit feminism in women's eyes, to discourage women from joining in the struggle, it is important first of all to claim that the movement's achievements are either insignificant or, when that's too difficult (such as with abortion) that they are the work of government, of political parties, of a sudden 'change' in 'mentalities' with no obvious cause. In short, that they are due to everything and anything except feminist struggles. This despoilment and these attacks do not only come from those who are the most evidently interested in keeping patriarchy alive. That would be too simple: just as it is relatively easy to defend oneself against these attacks precisely by showing the objective interests of one's aggressors. Aggressive actions are obviously all the more dangerous the further their origins are from the centre of the system and the closer they get to the movement.

It is no accident that the task of proclaiming the end of feminism is given to women – and to women who have a feminist *image*. It is easy to understand that the struggle is best discredited not by those who openly say that they are against women's liberation or against whose interests it obviously is, but by those women who claim that they are in favour of women's liberation, or in whose interests it would, objectively, appear to be. But there is a gap between the attacks à la Giroud[7] or à la Macciochi[8] (which even if they are part of an objective strategy are still the isolated initiatives of individual women) and an overall systematic offensive, carefully considered and put together, put into operation a long time ago, in fact since the birth of the movement. This is the *raison d'être* of the group *Psychanalyse et Politique*, of its founding the bookshop and publishing company *des femmes*. Its high point was reached and its aims revealed – in so far as they were previously hidden – with its attempt to own, legally (as it already owns in fact) the name Women's Liberation Movement.[9]

Its aims are even more ambitious than the ordinary kind of co-option described above: its goals are not just to steal the movement's achievements in order to use them against the movement. What they want, quite simply, is to steal the movement itself! In the face of such audacity, Giscard–Marchais–Giroud–LCR–Macciochi–LO etc.[10] (and I have deliberately left the list incomplete) seem like small-time operators, and their attempts even amateurish.

1980 will therefore also be a year of scandal, or rather the exposure of scandal. This scandal didn't just begin two months ago with the registration by *Psychanalyse et Politique*, a group originally part of the movement, of the title and logo MLF. This is only the latest stage in a long process of embezzlement; a long process in which nothing has been spared, least of all money, in the pursuit of the single goal of taking control of the women's liberation movement and putting it in the service of anti-feminism. This process could at first seem paradoxical; why choose the path that seems at first sight to be the hardest? It is really quite a long shot, like all projects marked by megalomania. But even this paradox has its advantage: we have to accept that its most contemptible aspect – their using the term 'women's liberation' against the goals of this liberation and against the women fighting for this liberation; you, me, all of us – is also the most effective: because it is this that has tied our hands, shut the mouths of women in the movement. It is precisely this aspect that has stopped the movement for so long – for too long – from denouncing this scandal.

Today we are resigned to the fact that we have to expose it, because it is no longer just the goals of the movement that are at stake, but its very existence. A movement that cannot appear as such can neither develop nor survive; a movement condemned to invisibility and to silence is dead. But was the existence of the movement not already threatened? Is the movement only defined as its 'present', made up only of the women who are 'in' it at any given moment? Is it not also and just as importantly a future, or at least the possibility of a future; and is this potential not precisely made up of all the women who are not yet 'in' it? And was this future not threatened when we let *Psych et Po* attack feminism in the name of the MLF?[11]

Haven't we forgotten this? Haven't we put this essential dimension of the movement – its future – in danger by allowing one group to appear as the whole movement in women's eyes? We must acknowledge that by not saying anything, we have been guilty of indifference towards what is said in our name, which is really a certain indifference towards other women. We have been guilty of a limited vision of the movement which actually contradicts the very idea of the movement. And this limited vision, this false definition of what a movement is, is incorporated in the formula which sums up the main reasons for our long silence: 'We mustn't wash our dirty linen in public.' The first flaw in this 'reasoning' is the belief that family secrets can remain secret indefinitely – even if we wanted them to, even if it was right to want them to. Everything comes out in the end.

But why did we want to keep this secret in the first place? We were afraid that by revealing what we knew and deplored (the devious actions of this group), we would weaken the whole movement 'because they are part of it'; we would 'be playing our enemy's game' who would be only too happy to draw general conclusions about all of us from it. We felt that the scandal of their actions would reflect badly on the whole movement. However we were wrong about this as well. Instead the opposite is true: if we don't expose what is happening first, if we let other people find out about it first, then the movement as a whole, and quite rightly, is held to be an accomplice. The devious actions will come to light sooner or later, and the later it happens, the greater our involvement. Whoever stays silent is giving consent, and whoever does not protest is giving approval – and the fact that this may all be done tacitly doesn't change a thing. Blame is always attributed just as much, maybe more, to those who cover up excesses as to those who commit them, because the former are guilty of dissimulation and duplicity.

We have already been corrupted by this duplicity with which we will be reproached, or rather with which we would have been reproached if we had continued to say nothing. By deciding to 'wash our dirty linen in private' we also accepted, without ever discussing or choosing it, the way that political parties and totalitarian regimes function; we accepted that which we condemn in traditional politics, in masculine parties; we accepted things that go against the principles of a liberation movement; we accepted the double standard: one truth for 'inside', another for 'outside'. The corrosive effect of this duplicity on individuals and on groups has been amply exposed and documented in the numerous accounts written by members and ex-members of the French Communist Party.[10] This lesson from history is not so far off that we have any excuses for not knowing about it – it is actually contemporary.

But most serious of all is the vision of the 'outside' of the movement and therefore of its 'inside', implicit in this behaviour. Because, after all, the women we are talking to – and who are we talking to if not to them? – *where* are they if not on the 'outside'? Why then are we reluctant to display our problems in public? Are we not showing contempt for these women by wishing to spare them this truth that we consider that *we* are able to cope with? Do we think that this truth that doesn't frighten us will put them off feminism? And what is so frightening about this truth for us or for other women?

What have we got to hide? What do we have to fear from the truth? In concrete terms here and now, nothing. On the contrary. And before? Maybe we wanted to present a 'unified' image of the movement. But that was a false image. Do we have so little confidence in women that we think that they will only be attracted by a lie? The problem doesn't arise any more. This 'value-conferring' image of the movement which has only ever existed in our heads (and we should know this because we have never stopped complaining about the media who don't present this image) will explode in the end. Either the *Psych et Po* scandal will break, and others will find out what there is to find out about that group and then the whole movement will be discredited by its passive complicity – or *Psych et Po* will succeed in representing the 'MLF' for all women (except for us, and to whom and how will *we* say it?), with the MLF saying that 'oppression has been overcome' and that women are 'above struggle'; replacing 'Let's fight together' with 'let's dance', and the MLF will become a movement against our liberation.

Today we have been given a fright: the appropriation of the term MLF has made us understand that the falsification of the past and the threat to the future are one and the same thing; that our past is not just photographs of the struggle but a terrain for struggle, because it is the condition of the struggle's continued existence. We must hope that this will teach us something and that we will not stop at that. We must understand that we are not only vulnerable to history but responsible for it: that by beginning a movement we undertook something not just for ourselves but for all women, present and future; that we can't say or even think 'after us, chaos'. A movement of oppressed people, whether it likes it or not, carries with it the hopes of all oppressed people. Whether we like it or not, we have a historical responsibility. For we, feminists of today, are accountable to the women of tomorrow; if we allow feminism to sink out of sight and disappear for the second time this century and if, having benefited – and suffered – from history and its manipulations, we do not do everything that is in our power to do in order to prevent them, in the year 2030 or 3017, having to start again from scratch, they will want to know why.

Today, telling the whole truth is the only way to save the movement. But what about yesterday and tomorrow? We have accepted, at least tacitly, the reactionary saying that 'it isn't always good to tell the truth'. This questions yet again our relation to the 'outside', that is to other women, and questions the nature of our movement, whether it is revolutionary or not. Ironically, we find ourselves in our present predicament, with the existence of the movement threatened, precisely because we have not told the truth. Perhaps we didn't think it was enough; or maybe we didn't think that it was necessary?

Against the lies of a system which, to guarantee a future without feminists, takes them out of the history of the present as it is written, we are trying to re-establish the truth. It is our goal. It is also our weapon, our only strength. But where will we find it, this power of the truth, if we only half believe it ourselves? If, imitating those in power, we use it in an opportunistic way – in other words, as a lie?

Our ability to convert our tries: to convert into achievements for the whole movement what struggle has taught one generation; to transmit our experience to others; to make it intelligible and illuminating to them; in short, to make it history – depends on our ability to show that for us 'it is always good to tell the truth' because truth is always revolutionary.

Notes and references

1   Georges Marchais is Secretary-General of the French Communist Party (PCF). The PCF claims to be the party for the liberation of women and denies the value of an autonomous women-only movement as divisive of the working class.
2   *Le Figaro* is a conservative French daily newspaper.
3   Madame Simone Veil was Giscard d'Estaing's Minister of Health from 1974 to 1978 and was responsible for drafting the abortion law and seeing it through Parliament.
4   *L'Humanité* is the PCF's national daily newspaper.
5   The manifesto of the doctors (Groupe-Information-Santé) came more than a year after the publication of the *Manifesto of the 343* women who publicly declared that they had had abortions at a time when it was still illegal. This first manifesto was a women's initiative, while the later intervention of revolutionary doctors and other mixed groups briefly took the abortion issue out of the hands of the women's movement.
6   Slogan used during the events of May '68.
7   Françoise Giroud, centre-left journalist on the weekly magazine *Express*, was appointed to the post of Secretary of State responsible for Women (*Secretaire à la Condition Féminine*) created by Giscard, but not having a budget or any power apart from 'making recommendations in favour of women'.
8   Maria Antoinetta Macciochi is an Italian politician and writer who lived and taught in Paris for three years. She is currently a Euro-MP. She proclaimed the death of feminism in 1978.
9   On 30 October 1979, *Psychanalyse et Politique* registered the name *Mouvement de Libération des Femmes* as their own name and company title.
10   There is an abundant literature on the rigidly hierarchical and secretive nature of the PCF. See, for instance, Jean Elleinstein, *Ils vous trompent, camarades*, Roland Gaucher, *Histoire secrète du PC*, André Harris and Alain de Sédouy, *Voyage à l' intérieur du parti communiste*, Henri Fiszbin, *Les bouches s'ouvrent*, Dominique Desarti, *Les Staliniens*.

PART TWO

Debates within the MLF

4 *Psychanalyse et Politique*: bringing 'woman' into existence

This group has already been mentioned several times. Women did not react indifferently to *Psych et Po* during the late 1970s, although the group has less importance nowadays. It attracted significant attention outside France, though, particularly in the USA and in Italy. Women were attracted to the theoretical stance that emerged from the group and also to the charismatic leader, psychoanalyst Antoinette Fouque, and to the writer/philosopher Hélène Cixous, who was for some time associated with the group. *New French Feminisms* went as far as to claim that *Psych et Po* exercised an 'intellectual terrorism' over other feminists in France. The group's influence and ideological stance clearly invite strong views and are seldom regarded with indifference. Its ideas are worth serious consideration, if only in order to understand what lies behind its actions, with which many feminists are in disagreement.

Psych et Po was one of the few groups in the MLF to construct a coherent theoretical position and try to develop a practice that was in harmony with the theory. As I see it, their theory derives directly from the work of psychoanalyst Jacques Lacan and his suggestion that 'woman', or 'femininity' is in radical contradiction with what he calls the Symbolic Order. The Symbolic Order is the series of signs, codes and rituals, expressed in language, that make up the terms with which we operate in society. Lacan suggests that as children resolve the Oedipus complex, they simultaneously acquire language and enter into the Symbolic. That is, they undergo an unconscious process whereby they become social subjects capable of functioning in our society. The Symbolic Order is founded on the Law of the Father, his authority, his name. It is therefore always patriarchal. Little girls, like little boys, enter into an external world and also into unconscious structures that are always patriarchal, controlled by masculinity: a girl's potential to be different – that is, to be herself – is never allowed to develop. In an interview with journalist Benoîte Groult, Antoinette Fouque says:

From the moment that she [a woman] begins to speak, to exist, she has to face problems which are all masculine and this is what puts her in mortal danger – if she doesn't use them, she doesn't exist, if she does use them, she kills herself with them. This is the fringe area where we are, and this is where we will lead the struggle. I think that historically women have never existed. The movement's goal is to bring them to existence as a differentiated space, a space for difference. Alterity is woman. (From *Le Quotidien des Femmes*, no. 9, 1975)[1]

Psych et Po's primary battle, then, was against the masculinity in women's heads: not against the material conditions of women's lives, nor against discrimination that can be changed through legislation, but, as feminist Nadja Ringart says in an article published in the daily newspaper, *Libération* (1 June 1977), against the 'phallus in our heads'. We have to understand what has turned us against our woman-ness; we must re-evaluate our own worth, celebrate our bodies, learn to appreciate and nurture the woman in us. *Psych et Po* sees certain strategies as essential to this end: psychoanalysis can help release our potential femininity; women-only spaces can provide the supportive, nurturing atmosphere in which our feminine selves can be encouraged to develop; we must move from seeking 'recognition by the Father' (the Father being authority in the shape of institutions or any established practice); we must rethink our values; we must redefine our sexuality and break with all dependence on men;[2] we must profoundly alter the way we think, the concepts we use, the language we use. We need a Revolution of the Symbolic. It is an impressive project, attractive in spite of the many reservations that pragmatic materialists like myself may have. It promises a different world, a different way of conducting human relations, and it promises that we can start to build this world now.

Dedication to the goal of creating this new world, bringing 'woman' into existence has, however, led to a practice that many feminists reject. Readers wishing to explore this rejection should refer to a collection, *Chroniques d'une Imposture*.[3] Readers wishing to explore the group's discourse and ideas should refer to *des femmes*'s former monthly and weekly magazines. The *des femmes* company published an occasional newspaper (*Le Quotidien des Femmes*, from 1974–6), followed by a monthly, glossy magazine (*des femmes en mouvements mensuelle* 1977–80) and later superseded by a weekly magazine (*des femmes en mouvements hebdo* 1979–82). None of these is still published.

The publisher and editor regret that permission was unavailable to reproduce translated texts that would have given non-French speakers a glimpse of the group's style and thinking, which involved a reassessment of language itself, and the desire to uncover a woman's language. We tend to assume that language is transparent, serving as a direct means by which to transmit our thoughts and ideas. Psych et Po's language makes us struggle with the texture of language, makes us question both meaning and syntax – what can and can't be said, the terms in which we frame our ideas. The language, deliberately, makes us uncomfortable.

The interview given by Antoinette Fouque to Catherine Clément of the socialist daily newspaper *Le Matin* was one of the rare occasions that she spoke in the mainstream press about the group that she had founded.

Notes and references

1 'Alterity' is another word for difference, implying radical 'otherness' as opposed to being different 'from' something else (in this case, different from men, which leaves men as the point of reference instead of banishing the point of reference).

2 *Psych et Po* rarely used the word 'lesbian', as they claim it 'demands the right to exist in a masculine world' rather than 'working for psychosexual maturity for women and thereby cultural subversion and Symbolic Revolution'.

3 Published by the Association du Mouvement pour les luttes féministes, 1981.

Interview with Antoinette Fouque*

The women's liberation movement (MLF) is going through a period of serious crisis. Women who, since 1968, had fought their battles together are today divided and in open conflict. The latest episode is the legal establishment of an association which is officially called MLF: this has never been done before. It was Antoinette Fouque, whose name – whose first name alone – has been associated with the MLF since the beginning and who was responsible for this action, an action which immediately provoked outrage from other women to whom it appeared to be an abusive and personal appropriation. Antoinette Fouque has agreed to talk to *Le Matin* about ten years of women's struggle, and to explain the reasons behind her gesture, as well as the reasons for the splits in the movement.

Le Matin What made you decide, today, to talk publicly when you are not used to the media and you work primarily using your own communications network – publishing company, weekly magazine, meetings?

AF It is the year of 'the historical'. I've just seen a programme on TV about the 1970–80 decade. Women's revolt was mentioned as something that can't be denied and is here to stay (after which, by the way, it wasn't mentioned again). The beginning of women's revolt, of the MLF, is said to be 1970. In fact – and this isn't an isolated historical point – this pseudo-origin is extremely ambiguous, extremely dubious. In 1970, the press reflected the existence of the movement for the first time: in an article in *L'Idiot International* and in reporting a demonstration (the placing of a wreath at the unknown soldier's tomb, for his wife). This dating of the movement set up the collusion of the media and the 'star system' using a few

Le Matin, 16 July 1980.

individual well-known 'names'. But this date hides the real genesis of the movement.

Le Matin Well then, when did this genesis really begin?

AF The first meetings took place in October 1968 in the wake of the May Movement which, after ten years of anti-imperialist struggles concerning Algeria and Vietnam, opened up a complex political situation and brought to the surface an additional contradiction – the sexual contradiction. During May–June, there hadn't been anything specifically to do with women: we were involved in 'agit-prop' at the Sorbonne. Mulling all this over took all summer, and in October we – that is, three women including myself – took the initiative of organizing women-only meetings: they were the first ones. At that time, we spent a lot of time justifying what we were doing: we had to make it clear that the MLF was born of the reactivation of the class struggle and chose to distinguish itself from, to break with, traditional feminism.

Le Matin What was the movement called in those days?

AF The movement had no name: we felt defensive about any kind of naming. Our first public appearance was at Vincennes in April 1970: about forty of us organized a demonstration and an open meeting without any links or subservience to any political party. 500 people came. It was a successful public coming out, even if the media failed to mention it. Those two years were fruitful – we worked on Marx, Freud, Lacan, on hysteria, on the specific contradiction of sexuality. We didn't impose it as the major contradiction, but we presented it as such. This was our historical intuition.

Le Matin Were there already splits in the movement?

AF Yes of course, or at least there were serious political differences which, after Vincennes, gave rise to two currents: feminism, whose practice involved 'spectacular' actions, and using women writers at the head – a practice of theatrical gesture. And us, people called us *Psych et Po* (psychoanalysis and politics), with our underground, anonymous practice: moles. We wanted *Psych et Po* to be a laboratory where we could try to understand the impasses of the May Movement and the women's movement (unexpected things that are not thought out occur in all movements as they develop). And to work on these un-thought-out aspects, we used the instruments of contemporary thinking, in particular psychoanalysis, which was the only discourse on sexuality that existed at that time. Then the term MLF began to circulate. The two currents continued to act separately and to do things together. However, the movement was, from the outset and without the women involved realizing it, caught in the two already existent clans – between Lacan and Sartre. On our side, we were never led, headed, patronized by anyone. Then women left their parties, their organizations. It spread, they joined us. From October 1970, before the FHAR (revolutionary homosexual movement), we affirmed the homosexuality of the movement: feminists, on the other hand, didn't yet say this. It was only later that they called themselves 'red dykes' or 'lesbians', still using provocation as their practice.

Le Matin   How long did this period last?

AF   At the end of 1973 we made a gesture, in order to declare our existence publicly: we founded the *éditions des femmes*. There had already been *Le Torchon Brûle* in 1971; it was produced by all of us in the movement, as was the event 'Days of Denunciation of Crimes against Women'. It was the era of many initiatives, bringing together all the currents.

Le Matin   In the present state of division and polemic that has split the movement, this would probably be impossible.

AF   It *is* impossible. But the shape of the movement is changing. It is particularly blocked in Paris, less so elsewhere. The difficulty was that many women believed – and still do – in the myth of unity: conflict between women is ugly, it's vulgar. Political difficulties should, therefore, have been stamped out. But we insisted on stating that we were not feminists, which meant, which means, that feminism is not the goal of our revolution. We are neither pre- nor antifeminist but post-feminist; we work for heterosexuality, to bring about the other, as Senghor was doing for Blackness – and he wasn't working against the White man. Contrary to what most people believe, our enemy isn't man but phallocracy; that is, the imperialism of the phallus. And there are men who have begun to understand that feminism is mostly 'up you get so I can take your place, in your phallocratic society without changing it'. What we wanted, what we have done, is to transform our condition of being 'excluded – interned' in this world, not through emancipation (included – interned) but through the effect of a 'great leap outwards' to independence.

Le Matin   And in 1979, you felt it necessary to create an association, MLF. This could have appeared as provocation to all women in revolt . . .

AF   By 1979 feminists had already abandoned the word 'liberation' for some time. MLF had become derogatory. We had moved into a period of repression, with International Women's Year (1975) and then the creation of a secretariat concerning women's condition and the re-burial of our achievement. Reforms are necessary but they imply paralysis of the movement. This paradox is difficult but it must be acknowledged.

We were saying in 1971 'no laws over our bodies'. And since then we've had the laws about abortion, about rape and about homosexuality. Therefore in October 1979 we, who had never rejected the term MLF – you find it in our texts, in our magazines, and in all the books we publish – we believed that there was a need, an urgent need, to give a minimum of anchoring, stability, to our movement.

Le Matin   A minimum of anchoring, but you still criticize institutions?

AF   You can't live in a perpetual state of negating institutions. The law on associations regulates political parties as it does local sports clubs: it is the most flexible form we could give to our movement. A movement, not an organization, not a party, but a form we have invented: yes, movement is the specific form of the art of revolution, which foils the totalitarianism of all-powerful political parties.

Le Matin   But why the need for a legal existence?

AF   There was the threat that the MLF would be effaced. We were in great danger. Rocard[1] was talking about 'incorporating' women and we couldn't just do nothing. Nor could we delegate our representation to a leader of a party, to the creator of some current, to some theoretician who turns herself into an institution. And then, because contradictions became divisions, the movement was threatened with dispersal, with self-destruction, with sterility. It is the moment to make links. We created this association in order to effect this symbolic liaison and this historic inscription. But it isn't a publishing company that has taken over a name: it is a movement which has, successively, created a publishing company, a monthly paper, a weekly paper, and has today created this association. Since 1968, a circuit of history has been accomplished. What we did in October 1979 was simply to assert an existence: it was a realistic action.

It is to make clear with a gesture that what I call the 'revolution of the symbolic' began with this movement; it is to project, to programme here, now, the beyond of the reality principle. Because we have to go beyond it, this reality to which we women have been subjected, up to feminist emancipation – which is as much of a travesty as femininity. We have to transform this reality, if it is based on the principle of the oppression by one class, race, sex over the others.

Notes and references

1 Michel Rocard is a prominent socialist politician and a potential rival to François Mitterrand for the socialist candidacy in the presidential elections of 1988.

5 Women's difference

In Great Britain, the question of whether or not women are innately different from men, and what the significance of that difference might be, has been generally dismissed by feminists as essentialism and does not find much currency except with feminists involved in psychology or psychoanalysis. In France, however, possibly because psychoanalysis itself reaches a wider and less sceptical audience, the question of women's difference has been one of the most controversial areas of feminist debate. *Psych et Po* were not alone in claiming for women an existence as 'other', as different *and* subversive. Many women have worked for the last ten years and more on the exploration of the notion that women have a different relation to language, to people and to thinking, from men:[1] and that it is not a question of life experience, but is something intrinsic to women.

Woman, woman-ness, femininity: these words are used to describe that difference, which derives, according to Annie Leclerc, author of the next extract, from women's bodies. Leclerc's book *Parole de Femme* was a prime example of a text that undertook the task of revaluing women's bodies, and of *writing* about women's bodies. She talks at length about experiences specific to women – periods, premenstrual tension, pregnancy, childbirth – she talks about the need to find an authentic woman's voice, not a male voice from within a woman's body, steeped as we are in the words of men, great thinkers – all men – fathers and husbands. Yet Leclerc's book ultimately seems to me to be a celebration of heterosexuality while claiming to speak of a different sexuality.

The body/language/difference connection, or theme, recurs not only in psychoanalysis but also in fiction, where it briefly received the name *l'écriture du corps* (writing the body). Writers associated with this exploration, rightly or wrongly, have included Chantal Chawaf, Hélène Cixous, Madeleine Gagnon and Xavière Gauthier, to name but a few.

The literary review *Sorcières* (sorceresses/witches) was one place where women wrote a 'Woman's Voice', taking each time a theme (blood, dolls, death), and the different writings around each theme show the diversity of women's experience and women's use of language. Difference, then, has found a niche in literary theory, which some women claim is profoundly political and can lead to more lasting change than the odd change in legislation.[2]

Other feminists have responded to the emphasis on women's bodies in a very critical way. In her article 'Protofeminism and antifeminism' Christine Delphy takes issue with Leclerc's lack of politics and with the way she abstracts the body from anything social:

When trying to 'revalue' our bodies, she uses only words which denote very physical things and acts: vaginas, childbirth, menstruation, etc. However, while there is certainly a physical, non-social element in our bodies and actions, there is also a social component. It is essential to recognize that the meaning of periods, for instance, is not *given* with and by the flow of blood, but, like *all* meaning, by consciousness and thus by society.[3]

The *Questions Féministes* collective developed a theory of women's oppression based on the notion of sex-classes: men as a class derive benefits from the oppression of women as a class. Colette Guillaumin, like Delphy a member of the collective, develops the idea of women as class-owned, appropriated by others, in her article 'The Question of Difference'. Guillaumin argues that the notion of difference contributes to perpetuating the status of women as a subordinate, subservient class. According to Guillaumin, difference does indeed exist – it exists in concrete, historical terms and must be considered in this way. When understood historically, difference is clearly shown to be synonymous with oppression.

The idea of difference, then, masks women's oppression, for Guillaumin. Even so, she concludes, difference contains a real consciousness of oppression, which we experience as conflict: conflict between our experience as subject – thinking, feeling human beings in our own right – and the way we are used as object. We experience this consciousness, this conflict, on an individual level, as our personal situation. Guillaumin calls for us to realize and acknowledge that it is not an individual problem but a social relation, a power relation, a class relation. She calls for us to build a collective consciousness in order to fight the oppression of difference.

Notes and references

1 See texts in *New French Feminisms* by Luce Irigaray, Hélène Cixous and Julia Kristéva. Translations of Kristéva's *About Chinese Women* have been made, translations of Irigaray and Cixous are forthcoming. See also the writing published in *des femmes en mouvements* magazines.
2 On feminist literary theory, see Toril Moi, *Sexual/Textual Politics* (Methuen, 1985). On feminism and language, see Deborah Cameron, *Feminism and Linguistic Theory* (Macmillan, 1985) and Dale Spender *Man-Made Language* (Routledge & Kegan Paul, 1980), My *Feminism in France* (Routledge & Kegan Paul, 1986), chapter 5, tries to unwrap some of the problems in the body/language/difference/politics chain.
3 Translated in *Close to Home* (Hutchinson, 1984), p. 195.

Woman's word*

Annie Leclerc

Nothing exists that has not been made by man – not thought, not language, not words. Even now, there is nothing that has not been made by man, not even me: especially not me.

We have to invent everything anew. Things made by man are not just stupid, deceitful and oppressive. More than anything else, they are sad, sad enough to kill us with boredom and despair.

We have to invent a woman's word. But not 'of' woman, 'about' woman, in the way that man's language speaks 'of' woman. Any woman who wants to use a language that is specifically her own, cannot avoid this extraordinary, urgent task: we must invent woman.

It is crazy, I know. But it is the only thing that keeps me sane.

Whose voice is speaking these words? Whose voice has always spoken? Deafening tumult of important voices; and not one a woman's voice. I haven't forgotten the names of the great talkers. Plato, Aristotle and Montaigne, Marx and Freud and Nietzsche. I know them because I've lived among them and among them alone. These strong voices are also those who have reduced me the most effectively to silence. It is these superb speakers who, more than any others, have forced me into silence.

Whose voice do we hear in those great, wise books we find in libraries? Who speaks in the Capitol? Who speaks in the temple? Who speaks in the lawcourts and whose voice is it that we hear in laws? Men's.

The world is man's word. Man is the word of the world.

No, no, I'm not making any demands. I am not tempted by the dignity of Man's status; it amuses me. When I consider Man, I am only playing.

*Extracts from *Parole de Femme* (Editions Grasset, 1974).

And I say to myself: Man? What is Man? Man is what man brings into the world. We made children, they made Man.

They turned the specific into the universal. And the universal looks just like the specific.

Universality became their favourite ploy. One voice for all. With one voice, only one can speak. Man.

All I want is my voice.

You let me speak, yes, but I don't want your voice. I want my own voice, I don't trust yours any more.

It is no longer enough to speak *about* myself for me to find a voice that is my own. Woman's literature: feminine literature, very feminine, with its exquisite feminine sensitivity. Man's literature is not masculine, with its exquisite masculine sensitivity. A man speaks in the name of Man. A woman in the name of women. But as it is man who has set out the 'truth' about us all, the truth about women, it is still man who speaks through woman's mouth.

The whole of feminine literature has been whispered to women in man's language. The whole range, all the melodies, of femininity, have already been played out.

Is it possible to invent anything new?

We have to invent: otherwise we'll perish.

This stupid, military, evil-smelling world marches on alone towards its destruction. Man's voice is a fabric full of holes, torn, frayed; a burned out voice.

However wide we open our eyes, however far we stretch our ears, from now on, the summits from where laws are made, male summits with all their sacred values, are lost in the thick fog of indifference and boredom. Which is when women open their mouths and begin to speak. From now on, no man's voice will come to cover up the multiple, vigorous voices of women.

But we still aren't there. In fact we won't get there unless woman manages to weave a fabric, whole and new, made of a voice springing from within herself. Because the voice can be new, but the words worn out. Watch out woman, pay attention to your words.

Let me say first of all where all this comes from. It comes from me, woman, from my woman's belly. It began in my belly, with small, slight, signs, hardly audible, when I was pregnant. I began to listen to this timid voice which had no words.

Who could tell me, could I ever express (and what words would I use), to speak of the extraordinary joy of pregnancy, the immense, terrible joy of childbirth.

That is how I first learned that my woman's body was the site of Dionysian celebrations of life.

So then I looked at men. For man, there is only one celebration of sexuality: intercourse. He doesn't want to hear about the others, the multiple celebrations of my body.

And this one celebration of his, he wants it all for himself. He demands that my necessary presence remain discreet and totally devoted to his pleasure.

Well it's too bad for him, but I must talk about the pleasures of my body, no, not those of my soul, my virtue or my feminine sensitivity, but the pleasures of my woman's belly, my woman's vagina, my woman's breasts, luxuriant pleasures that you can't even imagine.

I must talk about it, because only by talking about it will a new language be born, a woman's word.

I have to reveal everything that you have so determinedly hidden, because it was with that repression that all the others began. Everything that was ours, you converted to dirt, pain, duty, bitchiness, small-mindedness, servitude.

Once you had silenced us, you could do whatever you wanted with us, turn us into maid, goddess, plaything, mother hen, *femme fatale*. The only thing you demand really insistently is our silence: in fact, you could hardly demand anything more; beyond silence, you would have to demand our death.

It is our silence and the triumphant sound of your voice that authorized the theft of our labour, the rape of our bodies and all our silent slavery, our silent martyrdom. How can it be that we are now coming out of our coma, and that our tongues, though still sticky with respect for your values, are loosening up, slowly?

You had proclaimed the universality of your language. Very good for asserting your power, but not so good for keeping it.

We listen, convinced, to those who say 'All men are born free and remain equal in their rights.'

And slowly we discover that the person who has nothing, has the right to nothing. Not to equality, nor to freedom. And we end up by demanding the letter of the law. Equality. Freedom.

My body flows with the vast rhythmic pulsation of life. My body experiences a cycle of changes. Its perception of time is cyclical, but never closed or repetitive.

Men, as far as I can judge, have a linear perception of time. From their birth to their death, the segment of time they occupy is straight. Nothing in their flesh is aware of time's curves. Their eyes, their pulse, neglect the seasons. They can only see History, they fight only for History. Their sexuality is linear: their penis becomes erect, stretches, ejaculates and becomes limp. That which makes them live kills them. They escape death only by a new life that in turn, kills them again.

My body speaks to me of another sense of time, another adventure. Thirteen times a year, I experience the cyclical changes of my body. Sometimes my body is completely forgotten. Not thinking about its pains or its pleasures, I come, I go, I work, I speak and my body is an abstraction. Sometimes, my body is there, present.

Ten, twelve days before my period, my breasts swell, become hardened. This seems, in my case, to follow ovulation, fertility. I can't say that this is always so, because other women say they experience this during their period or just before.

The nipple is tender, bright red, very sensitive. The slightest contact makes it harder. You say, friends say to each other, 'My breasts are sore.' Especially if you are worried that your period is late, and you are looking for any hopeful signs, you weigh your breasts in your hands, feel them, press them with anxious care, trying to force them to admit that they hurt, you say, you repeat, oh yes, they are sore. But it's not that. They don't hurt, it's just that we can feel them. They are alive, aroused, open to pain but not sore. They are also open to caresses, much more so than usual; continually caressable, strangely open to pleasure. When my period is due, my breasts are loving, avid, sensitive.

I haven't finished talking about my body yet. For it experiences still more wonders. Just because you aren't involved with them, does it mean that I must hide them under a hideous mask of pain and suffering? Do I have to feel bad because I take pleasure in experiences you can't know, to the point of denying myself this pleasure too?

You have poisoned my life. For centuries. Deprived of my body, I only knew how to live through you. Badly, hardly living. Slaving away, enduring, being silent and being pretty. My body there for work and for pleasing you; never for my own pleasure. My body, never my own, for me. Mouth sewn up, face made up. Vagina open when you want it, closed up with Tampax. Scoured, scraped, made hygienic, deodorized and re-odorized with rose-smelling perfume, it's too much, it's stifling me, I need my own body. That is what I mean by living.

You could say, well what are women complaining about since you say there are so many possibilities for them to be happy? It is because these possibilities that we have here and now are merely an anticipation of what could be possible in a radically different society, in which woman's status would also be changed. As would the way in which she is perceived by others.

I'm not saying to women, be happy; but only, do you know that you are capable of happiness?

But we have to understand everything that denies women's happiness – and which is not only her economic, sexual and familial oppression.

We know full well, because it is glaringly obvious, that women are denied happiness because they are overburdened with domestic tasks and with anxieties that postpone their pleasure in life indefinitely, almost until her death. When does a woman really have the chance to take pleasure in herself, in man, in the sun, the rain, the wind, in children, in the seasons, even in the home, when she is constantly harassed by the need to take care of – the housework, the dishes, the washing, the shopping, the ironing, the cooking?

When can she even glimpse the possibility of happiness when, already rushed off her feet, she adds the hardship and humiliation of a badly-paid job? We can't pretend that we don't know about all this, because it can't be hidden, we can *see it*.

But do we know enough about what else denies a woman happiness, maybe even more radically? Do we know the extent of a tyranny we can't see – we can't see it because we can see neither the person exercising it nor how it operates, nor exactly on what it operates?

Do we understand that, excluded from her body, kept in ignorance about the pleasures it contains, it is the ability to experience happiness that is missing?

If women are so politically apathetic, so persistently conservative, is it not also because they are incapable of imagining what their pleasure in living could be?

The only bodily pleasure they are aware of missing is the one which they see men indulge in, more often and better than they do: a properly sexual pleasure. But is their imagination so limited that they can't think of other pleasures? Are they so shortsighted that they can't see the source of their problems? Are they too humble, too lazy? If only they learned to find in themselves those joys from which the world is cut off, would their struggle not acquire a new vigour and a new, indispensable rigour? If only they knew that, if man made this world which is an oppressive world, it is up to women to prepare the coming of a different world, which would at last be a world of life.

Women will not be liberated as long as they do not also want to be liberating, by denouncing and by fighting *all* oppression, those that come from man, from power, from work, but also those that come from themselves and operate on themselves, on others and particularly on their children: dis-incarnated women, de-sexualized women, disinfected, disaffected, glossy magazine women, puppet women, but also women who are men's accomplices, accomplices of the strong man, the husband, boss, cop, and also jealous women, capricious and vengeful, bourgeois women, mean women, finally and above all, women the dragon of the family, women martyrs of devotion, voracious mother-hens, possessive and murderous mothers, odious step-mothers.

As long as we are somehow in complicity with man's oppressions, as long as we perpetuate them on to our children, turning them into vigorous oppressors or into docile victims, we will never, never be free.

The question of difference*

Colette Guillaumin

In the good old days, a woman's worth was decided according to her animal qualities. The amount of her menstrual blood (this is important – a woman's value, like a milk cow's, is measured in litres); the number of children she has, her age at the onset of menopause.

In those days, we had no right to reproach men for competing over the size of their erections, because when it came to performance, we were just as bad. But all that was a long time ago, long ago, it's old history, dead and buried. We are not obsessed by our reproductive physiology these days, nobody cares about the number or the sex of her children any more, nor about her production of menstrual blood nor the age of menopause. That's all over, finished. We now carry off the rhythms of our femaleness with grace and consider these things simply as part and parcel of the normal circumstances of our lives.

The idea of difference, which is so popular among us at the moment – in France and elsewhere – is both heterogeneous and ambiguous. The one because of the other.

By heterogeneous, I mean that it covers both anatomical and physiological facts and also socio-psychological phenomena. This situation allows it to be used, consciously or unconsciously, at different levels, allows the concept to be used in whichever way is needed according to the circumstances at the time. It is ambiguous because it is a manifestation of false consciousness, and at the same time, it hides a (repressed) real consciousness.

Ambiguity guarantees the success of difference, because it allows antagonistic political feminist positions to join together in a superficial agreement. 'Difference' wins out, whichever way you look at it.

*From *Questions Féministes*, no. 6, 1979.

This article aims to look at the different levels of 'difference': these levels which are tightly linked, each resulting from the other, but which can each be analysed separately. I would like to show that difference is an *empirical reality* (i.e., it has a concrete existence and influence in our daily lives); that it is a type of logic (i.e., it is a particular kind of reasoning, a way to interpret what is going on, both in ourselves and around us, something in our heads); and that it is a *political attitude*, in that it presents itself as a set of demands and as a project (i.e., as something that affects our lives).

Finally, we can't talk about 'difference' as if it were a neutral term. We can talk about 'women's difference' as easily as we do because it's something that happens to women. Women are not milk cows (females) but a specifically determined social group ('women') whose main characteristic is that they are owned by others. They are appropriated as a group, not only as individuals trapped in a personal sense. This appropriation applies to all women, not just to some of us: owned by the father while a minor, by the husband or lover when a spouse. But all men (not just fathers and husbands) have 'rights' over all women and these rights are only limited when a woman is owned by a specific man. And finally, even when a woman has avoided being owned by one man, she still doesn't own herself.

What, in concrete terms, is difference? Things become a lot less clear here. These days, the demand for difference depends on the one hand on classical anatomical, physiological traits, well-defined and easy to see; from this perspective, what is different about women? Sex organs, weight, size, reproductive organs, speed. It also includes a whole range of emotions, habits and daily routine: attention to others, spontaneity, patience, sensitivity, the gift for making, and enjoyment of, jams, etc.

However the notion of difference also implies, while it hides, a number of factors which are more complex and removed from anatomy and subjectivity: use of space and time, longevity, the way we dress, salary, responsibility, social and legal rights. All in all, there is apparently as much difference between our world and men's world as there is between Euclidean geometry and curved air, between classical and quantum mechanics.

Let us take several, *supposedly superficial* (my emphasis is deliberate) examples of this famous difference: some of the things we wrongly thought were in the process of disappearing.

1 Skirts designed to keep women in a state of permanent sexual availability, making it more embarrassing for us when we fall (or just when we

are in awkward positions) and making us more dependent because we are more vulnerable in our balance and movement, which skirts insidiously guarantee. We have to pay special attention to our bodies, because the body is by no means protected by this clever piece of clothing, a kind of shutter hiding our sex organs and fixed to the waist like a lampshade.

2 High heels. We always pity Chinese women in history and we still wear stilettos, or very high heels, or something close to skates. These different shoes mean that we can't run, we twist our ankles, have to be extra careful when we have children or luggage or both with us, make us extra susceptible to grilles and gratings. They make sure that our independence is limited. I will, however, allow that they are better than having your feet bound: you can't take off your feet but you can take off your shoes.

3 Artefacts that grip our bodies – belts, waspies, suspender-belts, girdles – we don't wear corsets these days . . . but all these other things make it hard for us to breathe normally. Stretching is made difficult and upsetting. In other words, these things make sure that we can't forget our bodies. The veil, with its very clear meaning, is an extreme example of this. The difference is one of degree, not of nature, between all these instruments whose shared function is to remind women that they aren't men and they mustn't think that they are and they must *never* forget it.

4 Various loads and responsibilities (kids, shopping trolleys) also reveal our difference. A large number of women's movements outside the home are accomplished when burdened with these extra things, including going to work, because when you're a woman, every movement has to be useful, nothing wasted. Necessity is never justification enough for a woman's actions. She has to add usefulness to need, need to more need; shop on the way home, take the kids to school on the way to work, knit while watching the kids in the playground, peel vegetables during family discussions, make dinner while having her breakfast, etc. In other words, women never do only one thing at a time, and as far as possible, never have their arms free, their bodies free or their hands unoccupied.

Obviously I am comparing all this with men's activity, clothing and prostheses. I see all these men, no skirts, no high heels, empty hands, not knitting in playgrounds or in the metro, yawning (rather than criticizing it, I wish we could all be like that) and going home, maybe not exactly fresh, but at least not on their last legs and, at any rate, on flat heels.

These are all signs which many people consider trivial, but which are in fact very important. They express women's dependence – nobody can disagree with this point. But they don't stop at merely *expressing* it. They are also, and most importantly, techniques for keeping women dominated in the body and therefore in the mind. They do not allow women to forget what they are. And they provide women with a constant practical exercise in dependence maintenance. Wearing a clinging, short or slit skirt, very high pointed heels, or carrying a bag of groceries are some of the infallible ways to make us re-learn our difference, what we are and what we should be.

This reminder in our dress, our gestures, creates a very particular way of moving to which we have not yet paid enough attention.

5 The *smile*, always hovering at our lips, which automatically accompanies our slightest word, even our silence. Not always, and not all of us (as with skirts and high heels) of course, but only women, almost only women do it. The smile, which traditionally goes with submission and is obligatory in certain professions – hostesses, saleswomen – is also required of girl children, and women domestic servants. Demanded of wives and all women in inferior positions, it has become an automatic reflex. A reflex which always reminds us that we should give in, acquiesce, in all circumstances, and reminds us we are available and 'happy' to demonstrate our availability.

With the smile comes the zone of the ethereal, the halo where tenderness, spontaneity, warmth, grace, succour, etc. all create a mixed image, part geisha, part Virgin Mary, supposedly being the quintessential virtues of *Woman*. We are no longer required to have Rachel's qualities, qualities of a strong woman who guaranteed the comfort and luxury of her master: other qualities are demanded of us, but they are still 'different'. In this zone of the smile, of magic potions, even of less happy things like hysteria or poetic ability, we can find the current demand for 'difference', the right to be different, minority culture and its respectability – women's language, poetic or medical secrets, all-consuming passions, women's ways of doing things, from their table manners to their behaviour in bed, 'women's culture'.

We are in the bizarre situation of having something (difference) while demanding the right to have that very same thing. Which could make you think that either we haven't got what we have, or that someone wants to take it away from us. Yet the least alert, the least involved glance at our everyday lives shows that, on the contrary, difference is granted to us, given to us, even thrown at us, imposed on us! Everywhere and in every way. Well? What is all this about? How is it that different oppressed groups (not only women) at different times (not only now) demand 'difference'?

The expression 'the right to be different' was first used in the 1960s in international organizations and anti-racist movements first, and then in the media. I remember my disbelief. It was so clearly a political withdrawal by dominated groups (looked upon with great favour by those in power, hardly surprisingly). It was a reticence, or rather a refusal to analyse the problems of the legal struggle for integration.

Former colonies and Afro-Americans seemed then to have gained their civil rights. But these legal rights began to reveal that they were unable to produce *real* equality; the disparity between the hopes that inspired the struggles and the practical outcome of the struggles was too great. National, legal independence still isn't real independence, civil rights aren't *real* rights, constitutional equality isn't equality. For instance, legally we have the right to the same wages as men, but we *haven't got* the same wages.

We witnessed this kind of withdrawal during the 1970s. In other words, anxiety and the fear of having been had, blocked our political analysis: our analysis of the *relation* between the powerless and the powerful and the nature of that relation. To the point that many of us began singing sweet songs, and some of us began to whisper the word 'difference'. This graceful little whisper made such a noise that it may as well have been announced through loudspeakers. Suddenly we found ourselves surrounded by goodwill, and the powerful and the powerless each tried to shout it out the loudest.

The whole idea of minority 'culture' suggests that reggae, jam, soul music or maternal tenderness are in themselves justification for our existence. And even more, they are qualities, eternal, isolated qualities that have nothing to do with what produced them. We persist in thinking about them in isolation from what brought them about in the first place, and from what keeps them going, in material terms, in daily life. For there is no maternal tenderness without childcare, no jam without domestic relations, no reggae or soul without unemployment.

It is striking that demands for a 'culture' join the tolerance of the powerful to the impotence of the powerless. Calypso or creativity are greeted by the amused, more or less condescending, interest of the powerful. What is it about these demands that makes them consonant with the interests of the powerful, so that they don't get angry at certain cries? He who has the material means to control the situation (even though there are sometimes abrupt jolts in this control) can well accommodate these cultural demands, more or less messianic visions, which don't threaten them by trying to find concrete ways of gaining independence.

What then happens that seems so dangerous in their eyes that it transforms paternalistic permission and interested (or amused) smiles into menaces and then to force? Isn't the search for, and the achievement of, practical, concrete *means* to gain independence, the turning point? The harshness of conflicts in this field, whether collective or individual conflict (in divorce, for instance) shows that what the powerful fear more than anything else, is the actual, or simply the future, *autonomy* of the powerless.

All our 'specific' characteristics are thrown, pell-mell, into this word, 'difference'. So difference joins other 'folklore' ideologies, which, from Black specificity to women's specificity have always claimed that the dominated – themselves – have something specially their own, and that everything their own is special. (The others – the dominant – are no doubt happy with just being ordinary.)

In the end, behind all this, there is the vague notion of the sexes defined in terms of *Being*. 'Femininity' has a sort of existence all of its own, and has nothing to do with social relations. Nor has it anything even to do with supposed 'natural' relations: for if the human race is anatomically and physiologically sexually differentiated, it implies precisely that womanness by itself can't exist any more than man-ness in itself (funnily enough, no-one seems interested in this last error, no-one cares about 'male reality'). The sexually differentiated nature of the human race, the fact that it is a species whose reproduction is sexual, implies, by definition, that the species is *one* and that there are not two kinds of human beings.

But let's leave aside the 'natural' – an ideological–social construct anyway – and let's think about the fact that human societies consider that that they are divided into men and women. This is all quite right except in the way that these two groups exist. It's true that there are two social groups, two classes born from a social relation and whose social existence is hidden by the anatomical–sexual division.

Somehow we have the crazy hope that men will decide to stop dominating and using us, that they will make this altruistic decision themselves, that they will 'acknowledge' us, that they will *give* us permission to emancipate ourselves – they will not only give us our freedom, but also their love. And they will do this, we believe, because if we are not 'like them' but 'different', then they have nothing, nothing at all, to fear from us, from what we will or can do. In thinking difference, *we* think 'we won't hurt you, so leave us alone'. In thinking difference, *they* think 'they will stay in their place'.

The demand for 'difference' is the expression of the fact that we are defenceless, and, furthermore, we don't want to defend ourselves, nor gain the means to do so, but all we want is respect and love. In fact, this amounts to a demand for weakness. But – can the demand for weakness and dependence eliminate the reality of dependence and weakness?

But we can also see this demand as a political, or at least a proto-political, protest? If, on the one hand, it may be a tactical error in that it serves dominant interests rather than helping us discover our own, if it may also be a manifestation of false consciousness, its ambiguity also makes it something else. It is quite probable that a 'misunderstanding' explains the success of 'difference'. While it is a heaven-sent gift for men, it is at the same time a *compromise* for many of us: a compromise between the emergence of a political consciousness of the fact that we really do form a class of women, and repression of this awareness. So our political awareness is both repressed and expressed by the notion of difference. So then difference is also the beginning of real consciousness; our own consciousness, that we hesitate at because its implications are frightening: it can make us realize that we form a social class. Because in fact we are different. *But* it isn't that we are different *from* men, as false consciousness would have it, but we are different *from what men claim that we are.*

This surely not coincidental coincidence of two meanings (we're different from you *and* we're different from what you say we are) has meant the success among women of a politically disastrous idea.

The emergence of a consciousness that makes us know ourselves as different from what we are supposed to be comes from something that we cannot *not know*, somewhere, even buried deep within us: we are *used*, and from the use made of us comes the violence that surrounds us and the contempt that encircles us. I use the words violence and contempt, this contempt that deep down we can't accept because it implies that we are . . . No! we are other, we are different, we are not that! I am not even talking about hatred, so intense, because while hatred is physically destructive, contempt is psychologically destructive: it denies us our self-respect (which we know), but it also deprives us of our intellectual and political strength by trying to make us accept and internalize the status of appropriated object.

So we censor ourselves, we pretend, we say something else, we say that we love children, we love peace, we say we don't give a damn about power – although we never exactly say what we mean by 'power', as if it was an object that you can take or leave, something in itself – *as if it wasn't a relationship*. In fact it isn't so obvious that we accept not being paid, doing all the work, being subjected to sexual violence or harassment etc., as easily as all that. Nor is it true that we accept finding ourselves without any means of a real response.

No, we stay rather vague, without defining either 'power' or 'difference'. What goal does this demand (for difference) have in mind, remaining unformulated as it does about its aims and the shape it could take? On the one hand, there is feminine mystique, or neo-femininity; on the other, the rejection of 'power' (did anyone ever actually offer us any?), horror of violence and contempt.

Dif-ference

So let's talk about the right to be different, about the fact that people think it would do us an injustice not to recognize our difference that we feel so strongly and that we feel is our own territory, our freedom in the face of their constant encroachments on us.

First, a little etymological comment that may be useful (those who say that words don't mean anything are either hypocritical or desperate), for no word is chosen accidentally. *Difference* comes from the Latin verb *fero* which means 'to carry', 'to direct'. Dif-ference adds the idea of dispersion (*di*) to that of direction; we say 'differ *from*'. The importance lies in the *from*. You can, of course, talk about difference *between* one thing and another, in which case each term is the reference for the other. This is an unusual use of difference. The usual meaning is that of distance from a centre, distance from a point of reference. In practice, you can claim that we mean 'X and Y are different from each other', but in *fact*, we say 'X is different from Y'. We place Y in the position of referent. While language offers us the chance to make egalitarian statements (between), it is still hierarchy (from) that is the rule.

So, difference can be thought of first, in a relation, but second, in a particular type of relation, where there is a fixed point, a centre which organizes everything around it and by which things are measured; in a word, a *Referent*. This is in fact the hidden reality of difference.

The ideological significance of difference is this distance from a referent. To speak of 'difference' is to speak of a rule, a law, a norm. In other words, it means to speak of an absolute which is the measure, the origin, the fixed point of a relation – in terms of which the rest is determined. It assumes that there is, somewhere, a fixed entity. And this amounts to assuming that there is no reciprocal action. It is simply the statement of the *effects* of a power relation. There is a great degree of realism hidden in the word 'difference': the knowledge that there is a source of evaluation, a point of reference, an origin of the definition. The definition of difference presents itself as precisely what it is – the fact of dependence and the fact of domination. And from this comes, logically, the idea of a 'right' to be different.

A right, whether in fact or in law is something that is defined *in relation to* something. In relation to a rule, a norm, a tradition. So by definition, a right refers to power. A right is *gained* and is therefore located in a perspective of dependence, of being granted – not in one of negotiation or exchange.

A member of the dominant group would clearly never demand the 'right to be different', first, because his practices and his ideal existence are in fact the social norm – and second, because he thinks of himself as an exquisitely specific and distinguished individual within his group. And he exercises this distinction as his right without asking, nor having to ask, for authorization from anyone, individuality being a practical effect of being dominant. The 'right' to be different, on the other hand, asks for authorization. Please give us the right to be *other* than you. Or rather, more clearly: you are the centre of the world. This suggestion amounts to saying 'You are the Law'.

The 'right to be different' does not occur in the context of an undifferentiated relation, a neutral world. When do we actually talk about the 'right to be different'? In the relations between the 'developed' world and the exploited world, in what we call 'race' relations and 'sex' relations? It concerns specific human groups who have a precise relationship between them, namely a relationship of domination and dependence. They are groups whose relationship is such that the first group derives its substance from the other, and the existence of the other is at the mercy of the first one's power. To speak of the 'right to' is somehow, somewhere, acknowledging the status quo of the power relations to which we are subjected. It is acknowledging the existence of these relations which is different from knowing them. We accept them because we don't know them, which puts us in a lousy position to fight and destroy them.

Contrary to what we are usually told, it isn't a question of an alternative between 'different/same'. It isn't a question of choosing, because our place is predetermined as that of difference. No choice. The visible dichotomy hides what is done to us, women, made into tools, instruments for the survival or the pleasure of the dominant class, men. There is no choice in this relationship. When they try to make us believe that there is, they treat us like a child, whose pain and rage is defused by directing it towards something else ('oh, look at the pretty flower!') so that, absorbed in something other than its pain, it won't see it any more, forgets it – and finally the object of its pain disappears altogether.

There is not, therefore, a different/same alternative which it is possible for us to face. They form the two sides of the same power relation. Unless we adopt a mystical point of view and side with the famous argument that claims that freedom is choosing the situation that has been imposed on you (slaves are therefore free), the idea of choice is absurd.

Let's take, for instance, our material existence and let's see how 'difference' is a concrete relationship: the wage scale.

We know, for example, that the pressure to marry (that is, the passage from collective appropriation to private appropriation – or from one private owner to another) involves the wage scale. We know that the relation between women's wages and that of the head of a family not only pushes women to marry and allows men to acquire a unit that gives his person physical and emotional comfort, but also (statistically) leads women to accept men who are older than them. The hierarchy that gives the best wages to older men and the lowest to women (whatever their age), is a coherent mechanism which gives 'mature' men private use of young women. As a result, there aren't two scales (one of age and one of sex), but only *one*, continuous, scale, which only becomes visible when we put sex-classes in the centre of the picture.

1 This scale comes from, and guarantees, the physical and material upkeep of one class, men (and men's children), by another class, women. This means, as we see more and more clearly, material upkeep itself: from shopping to cleaning, from cooking to supervising children, from

keeping social links going – family, professional, worldly or simply friendly – to being men's ornament in society.

2 As a result, women are deprived of the material means of existence in their mature years and in their old age. Abandoned, divorced, they are excluded from social rights (sickness benefits, pension) as soon as they are no longer private property. Forced into unemployment or reduced to receiving social security, which might be ('might' doesn't mean 'will') about 1000 francs a month (in 1978), women are deprived of the means of existence in the most material and immediate sense when they return to the status of being subject only to *collective appropriation*. They are reduced to begging in its truest meaning. They haven't got the right to any of the things that they had had when owned by one specific man: not only the things paid for by men's money but the rights that are (theoretically) guaranteed by the community to each of its members are taken away. This shows only too clearly that a woman isn't a member of the community; she is only her husband or lover's property. A woman, as woman, that is, without her own income, has no individual rights, no existence as a social subject.

A number of 'womanly qualities' follow on from this, qualities that can be thought of as unique and precious, pleasant or exciting: 'feminine qualities' which find their niche in the famous 'difference'; ties between human beings, invention in daily life, attention to others (although, between ourselves, we would prefer attention to others to be shared out a little more fairly). Praised as such, these qualities are the results – happy, value-conferring, inestimable – but results all the same of a material relation, of a certain situation in a classic relation of exploitation.

Unless of course we believe (conveniently and reassuringly) that 'whims', tenderness, jams, are written into women's genetic code which thereby shows – an interesting novelty – that it is distinct from men's; and that we are talking about our nature. In which case we would be right to defend it fiercely against anyone attacking or meddling with 'our' genetic message and trying to turn us into men, against our will.

Into 'men'? There are two important things here:

1 We have subtly changed terrain here, by ideological slips and a vocabulary that traps us. Now we are talking about females and males, not about women and men – which isn't the same thing, although they constantly try to make us believe that it is. In the one case, we're talking about

physical characteristics required for sexual reproduction: all species who reproduce themselves by mating have a female and a male sex and human beings are no exception – there are both females and males. When we talk about women and men, we are talking about social groups who maintain a predetermined relation and who are in fact constituted within this relation by specific practices. These practices concern the entire life of each of these individuals and organize their existence. from work to the laws that govern their lives, from clothes to the possession of the material means of survival, etc.

2 However, and we mustn't forget this, we don't need to defend ourselves against any aggressive act which tries to take away our young children, our tenderness, our imagination or the soap powder that washes whiter. On that score, we can go as far as to say that everything works together to make sure we keep these privileges and the practical means to cultivate these exquisite qualities. There is not the slightest danger on the horizon. No, they won't take away our kids, our old people, family, washing and house-work, nor our cooking or the way we listen to men's personal, professional, political and emotional problems. They will not take away the things that cause the 'negative spots' of difference: hysteria, mythomania, anger, fatigue, despair, madness. No, they won't take away the constant control exercised over us at home and on the street. Nor will they deprive us of harassment, nor the unfathomable egocentricity of men. They won't take away the uncertainty with which most of us exist: Will he come back? Drunk or not? Will he stay? Will he give me money? They won't deprive us of silence nor of the decisions they make about us. No, we mustn't get all worked up over an imaginary fear, they won't take away the things that make us different; we mustn't waste our time asking for what we already have.

The 'difference' demanded is supposed to confer dignity on those who, in our society, don't have any. Unfortunately, dignity isn't only made in our heads, but in *reality*. So, believing that demand for esteem and respect guarantees us this esteem and respect is dreaming awake: have you forgotten Mother's Day? And the campaign to 'rehabilitate' manual labour? Let's talk about this campaign, where manual labour was photographed and put on enormous posters all over town, was represented by miners' helmets, mechanics' hammers, builders' boxes, cranes and men's faces. Manual labour isn't feeding a number of people, doing the laundry, chang-ing and washing the baby, cleaning the shelter of a family group, oh no, that's not manual labour, that's woman's mission in life – watch out for the nuances. But manual labour apparently is not piecing together garments, soldering an electric circuit, binding books, sorting fruit – not one woman's face appears. Only men do manual labour. What is more, what this campaign reminds one of more than anything is the appalling worker's medal, and the emotional comments on good and faithful servants, loved in their place and not anywhere else. Our place is difference; no-one denies it to us, they will even praise it at some reception–ball–party celebrating the good little woman or the medal-holder at some festival for procreators. And even when we're past procreating, they have a place for us: when we're old, we can still do 'small' tasks, where we are irreplaceable as grandmothers, housekeepers or servants within the family. It is really only when we can only 'look after' ourselves (not anyone else) that we are thrown out of the system, to join the old people who, in their total impotence, weigh down a society that moans constantly about the expense they represent and the pressure they put on national finances.

To claim that difference is admirable is to accept the perennity of exploitation. It is for us to think in terms of 'eternity'. And, maybe more seriously, it is not to see that we are in a relation of exploitation ourselves, accepting the idea that nature is nature. Or maybe it's being so desperate that we pretend that it is. And this would be what we've learned over our long experience: don't make too many waves or we may eventually lose everything. Play silly, play the child: it is more acceptable to satisfy our whims than to settle our account. Or we can play sturdy, play the fool, the good woman, the eternal woman. Or again, the diplomat, the reasonable woman, the one who won't go too far, who won't ruffle the delicate sensibility of the master who is so fragile – so fragile.

But history doesn't stand still. Fighting for the establishment of relations that, by definition, cannot be the same as those which exist today – because these are the ones we are destroying – gives us the chance to do something new.

While domination divides us, because of the combined effects of the use made of us and the internalization of our 'difference', it also spawns our consciousness. The way that the practices of the dominant class cut us into bits, makes us think of ourselves as formed of odd bits and pieces. In our patchwork existences, we have to experience things that are distinct from each other, and isolated from each other, and so we act in an accordingly fragmented way. But our real, our own, existence, hidden behind this fragmentation, is constantly reborn in our sense of our bodies and in our awareness of its unity. Our resistance to the way we are used (resistance which increases as we analyse it) gives our existence coherence.

But even if it is – or maybe because it is – full of conflicts created in us by the use made of us at every moment in our daily lives, our consciousness is the expression of these conflicts. If we are torn apart and if we protest, it is because somewhere in each of us, the subject is discovering that she is being used as an object. Constant anguish, so constant in our lives that it is boring and banal, is how we express this tearing apart: knowing that we (me), who are thinking subjects in our own practice, are denied as subjects in the social use that is made of us.

The conflict between the subject (that is, the experience of our own practice) and object (that is, the appropriation that chops us into pieces) produces our consciousness. Today, this consciousness is often an individual, a particular, experience, and is not yet shared as class consciousness. In other words, it is a consciousness of ourselves as individuals, but not yet the knowledge that we are defined by a social relation and that it's not an unhappy coincidence or personal bad luck that has put us into this unbearable dilemma.

It is time that we knew ourselves for what we are: ideologically dispersed because we are put to dispersed concrete uses. But, as an appropriated class, we are unique and unitary. As women conscious of our dispersal by power relations, separating us, distancing us, differentiating us, we are struggling for our class, our own life, which can't be divided.

6 Radical lesbianism: politics and/or sexuality?

In February 1980, *Questions Féministes* (QF) published two articles which sparked off a serious dispute, first inside the QF collective and subsequently in the MLF as a whole. These two articles dealt with the question of lesbianism as a political choice for feminists: as the logical political choice for feminists. Monique Wittig in '*La Pensée Straight*' (Straight Thinking) attacks heterosexuality as the normative and oppressive structure underlying all institutions and all thinking, all concepts. Wittig takes issue with the language of the social sciences and the categories that are established: for instance, man, woman, sexual difference, the unconscious, culture and history. Wittig attacks the tendency to think in terms of a universal and global truth. She says that the consequence of this is that 'straight thinking cannot imagine a culture, a society in which heterosexuality not only organizes all human relations but also the way it produces concepts.'[1] Wittig goes on to raise themes that she continues in her later article '*On ne Naît pas Femme*' (One is not born a Woman)[2] which places lesbians outside the categories 'man' and 'woman'. In that article, she contends that what constitutes a woman is 'a particular social relation with a man, a relation that implies personal and physical obligations as well as economic obligations . . . a relation that lesbians escape by refusing to become, or to stay, heterosexual.'[3] 'Straight Thinking' concludes by saying that 'lesbians are not women'.[4]

The second article in the February 1980 issue of QF was by Emmanuèle de Lesseps, called '*Hétérosexualité et Féminisme*' (Heterosexuality and Feminism). She argues against political lesbianism on several counts, rejecting the idea that feminism should exclude heterosexual women, and saying that no one kind of feminism is the best. She discusses the notion of choice as it is presented in political lesbianism, and then defends heterosexuality as being subject to as much normative control as homosexuality. Lesseps acknowledges the contradictions that all heterosexual feminists face, but dismisses the idea that feminism must abolish contradiction, believing rather that it must face women's reality, and that most women are heterosexual. Impossible, argues Lesseps, to turn feminism – which after all grew directly out of women's lived experience – against women, by defining heterosexual experience as nothing but oppression and labelling heterosexual women as collaborators.

Following the publication of these two articles, tensions within the QF collective made working together impossible. Upon the dissolution of the collective, both sides signed an agreement not to use the same title for any future publication. Then the radical feminists on the collective (as opposed to the political – or radical – lesbians) produced *Nouvelles Questions Féministes* which was felt by the other women to be a betrayal of the agreement. The reasons behind the split and the subsequent animosity are not clear, as the women involved say themselves. A lot of the anger exploded at a meeting called in Paris by a group of radical lesbians during which heterosexual women were called 'collaborators' and lesbians who continued to defend them and to work with them were called 'kapos' (prisoners in concentration camps who helped the guards).[5]

In the beginning, the central issue was (and the main difference continues to be) whether or not feminism and heterosexuality are compatible; but other issues were inevitably drawn in. At the heart is clearly the relation of sexuality to politics (the personal to the political?), the nature of oppression, the nature and the goals of the women's movement and whether or not it is acceptable to suggest that there is one, correct, way in which to fight as a feminist. Is the women's liberation movement for all women or is it reserved for those who have 'got it right'?

This whole debate has been within radical feminism, as other feminisms have remained generally heterosexual in their thinking and in their image, if not in individual women's personal practice. Both sides of the QF collective claim to be logically continuing the radical feminist premise that women and men form two sex-classes with antagonistic interests. Men, whether they want to or not, derive objective benefits from women's oppression. Feminists, fighting for an end to women's oppression, cannot, according to radical lesbians, maintain close personal and sexual relationships with men without collaborating with the oppressor. Heterosexuality is identified as a political strategy which perpetuates men's power over women; heteroppression is at the core of society and is evident within the women's movement, they argue, as well as outside.

The radical feminists also claim to be continuing their own logic and, for them, the radical lesbians have departed from the original QF position.[6] They argue that lesbian oppression is a form of women's oppression – you don't escape, as Monique Wittig suggests, by being a lesbian. The radical feminists also reject the vanguardism implicit in political lesbianism: the women's liberation movement is for all women, not just for some.

The QF split is documented in this section from both sides of the argument: on the radical feminist side, there is an extract from the editorial of the first issue of *Nouvelles Questions Féministes*, first translated and published in *Trouble and Strife*, no. 2 (1984); on the radical lesbian side, there is an extract of a letter to the feminist movement, distributed at a meeting in Paris on 8 March 1981, when the radical lesbians decided not to identify with, or work with, the MLF any more.

The remaining texts move the debate away from the focus on QF, and explain the political positions held by radical lesbians (two short tracts, distributed at meetings) and by radical feminists (both homosexual and heterosexual) from *la Revue d'en Face*. Any real dialogue or engagement between the two sides of the debate seems now to be impossible, as two different definitions of lesbianism are operating. Political lesbians are saying that lesbianism is not a form of sexuality but a political strategy; opponents attack the notion of a hierarchy of correct radical behaviour within the women's movement and the idea that sexuality, as individual sexual relationships, is an expression of politics. The radical feminists argue that heterosexual relations are a site of struggle and that lesbianism without feminism leaves patriarchy intact.

Notes and references

1　Monique Wittig, *Questions Féministes*, no. 7, 1980, pp. 49–50.
2　Monique Wittig, *Questions Féministes*, no. 8, 1980.
3　ibid., pp. 83–4.
4　Monique Wittig, ibid., p. 53.
5　See 'What's the French for "political lesbian"', in *Trouble and Strife*, no. 2, 1984.
6　See Editorial of *Questions Féministes*, no. 1, 1977, translated in *New French Feminisms*.

Extract from editorial of *Nouvelles Questions Féministes**

Exit *Questions Féministes?* Not really, for here is *Nouvelles Questions Féministes,* whose aim is to continue the work that *Questions Féministes* did for three years. Let us make it clear: the change of title in no way indicates a change of direction or of content.

Questions Féministes succeeded in being what it set out to be: the place for theoretical debate which was so badly needed in the feminist movement. We therefore owe our readers, and the movement in general, an explanation for the split in our editorial collective; even though it's true to say that we don't fully understand it ourselves.

The QF collective split up in June 1980 over the issue of the 'radical lesbian' position put forward by a group which was then known as 'the Jussieu lesbians'. Starting from a critique of heterosexuality as the site and the central means by which women are oppressed, this position ended up calling heterosexual women 'collaborators' – a formulation which provoked violent arguments within the heart of the movement. According to this position, if women and men constitute two antagonistic classes, it follows that all contact between the classes is 'class collaboration', and for those of the oppressed class this is a betrayal of themselves.

One half of our old collective declared they were, on the whole, in solidarity with the position. The other half, ourselves, reacted against it strongly – or, more exactly, we reacted against the 'conclusion'. We felt it was incompatible with the principles of feminism and with the theoretical and political orientation of the journal. We believed the conclusion contradicted the premises of radical feminism: i.e. the recognition that women, all women, constitute an oppressed class; that we are all oppressed by men as a class; and that feminism is the struggle against this *common* oppression of

*No. 1, March 1981; translated by Sophie Laws.

all women. The term 'collaborators' denotes political enemies, not those who share one's oppression, not allies. And collaborators cannot, by definition, at the same time be resisters, that is, feminists.

The two sides of the collective evaluated the role and importance of this 'conclusion' very differently. For the other side, the critique of heterosexuality was the base, while the condemnation of heterosexual women was a 'form'. They said they were against this condemnation, but refused to discuss it precisely because they said it was a problem of 'form' and not of content. According to their logic, wanting to discuss the condemnation of heterosexual women was 'making technical criticism to avoid talking about the main point'. As necessary as is a critique of heterosexuality, no theoretical necessity can justify exclusion of any woman from the oppressed class, from the class of women. We reject the obligatory linking of a critique of heterosexuality with the condemnation of heterosexual women.

1 A split, therefore, appeared in the very form of the discussion, which, although it was not over the 'basic point', was just as serious in our eyes as the split over the definition of feminism. It was the problem of intellectual terrorism, and ultimately of totalitarian thinking. The 'radical lesbians' presented their position *en bloc*. One might not criticize it. Either you were totally with them or totally against them. If one criticizes the condemnation of heterosexual women, in their eyes this means that one refuses to criticize heterosexuality, or even that one is 'defending heterosexuality', that one is upholding a 'radical heterosexual line'. We refused to accept this type of argument, not only because it is specious, but, more seriously, because it is terrorism. Historically this way of thinking is well known. It generally justifies a totalitarian practice, but unfortunately it is not restricted to dominant groups or to established regimes and it is not a male prerogative either. We have seen a totalitarian system among women in this country with the *Psych et Po* group.

2 The logic of the 'radical lesbian' position ends up with the purging of heterosexual women from the feminist ranks, as their texts explicitly say.

3 Since the simple exclusion of heterosexuals from the movement is obviously an impossible task, in reality, their position means bringing a vanguard theory into feminism (with radical lesbians as the most advanced feminists).

4 So what then caused the split in QF? For us, the internal history of our group and its conflicts, either personality, role or power conflicts (as with

every other group) provides the rest of the story. But, strangely enough, the other side denies that these factors played any part in their actions in regard to us. They claim that their actions were 'purely political'.

Even this denial was based, we think, on a very different idea of the relationship between the personal and the political from ours. Three of the other side refused to discuss their personal lives within the group. We said that it would be extremely worrying individually and a handicap from the point of view of consciousness-raising and theoretical analysis if we discussed subjects like heterosexuality and lesbianism without reference to our 'private lives'.

Their refusal to be open reduced their politics to 'the personal should be political'. Put differently, it means the 'the political is not about analysis and strategy, it is about your personal lifestyle'. Their politics started not from the personal, but with assertions about how one ought to live, with accusations which made women feel guilty if they didn't live up to the proposed ideal. They said and say that the ideal should and must, here and now, be made material in each individual feminist's life. They want to abolish the objective contradictions between women's ways of life and their politics, and to transform women's lives into 'hard politics'. They insist women's whole beings should express the 'correct line'. Their aim was and is, therefore, not to fight against oppression but to express non-oppression.

In 1977 (when QF was begun), of all points at issue, one did actually seem to us to be settled and agreed among the collective and not in need of further discussion. This was the thesis that women constitute a class. But we can now see that without agreement on other points, even this theory whose strategic implications were so clear, could be turned around, perverted in the strong sense of the word (that is, turned against itself). The absence of agreement on other points made it possible to slip in, after the proposition that women are a class, a series of intermediate statements which replaced the conclusion that men are the main enemy, with one which said that women are the main enemy.

Not only must criticism of heterosexuality be dissociated from the condemnation of individuals, of heterosexual women, but this dissociation is central to radical feminism.

Letter to the feminist movement*

Lesbian radical feminists from the ex-*Questions Féministes* collective

The editorial collective of *Questions Féministes* was dissolved on 24 October last year, as was the association linked to it. The journal is therefore not published any more; the last issue was supposed to be no. 8 (May 1980). The ex-collective split into two groups, with opposing interpretations of political conflict. It is regrettable that it was not possible to express these differences in a final issue of *QF* which we could have put out together, and which would have allowed our readers to see, *clearly set out*, what was at stake in the conflict and the terms of the conflict. Instead of this explanatory issue, there are rumours, caricatures and exclusions, which hide the real debate. Recently, part of the ex-collective announced the publication of a journal called *Nouvelles Questions Féministes. We demand that this title be withdrawn* because in October, all the women in the collective signed a *written agreement* that none of them would use the title *Questions Féministes* for a new journal. Both parts of the collective still claim that they are in line with the editorial of *QF* [which set out the basic 'radical feminist' position in 1977], and with its political aims. To use this title, as those women putting out *NQF* are doing today, is to set themselves up as the only holders of the 'correct QF line'.

The split within QF was the direct result of a debate, or rather of a political conflict *within the movement*: that is, the question of lesbianism and heterosexuality in relation to feminist political commitment. This conflict became most acute in Paris from March 1980 onwards, but was not just a Parisian debate. This question has been raised everywhere, elsewhere in France where there are lesbian groups and journals, and in other countries. It is not a new debate, it has been present since the

*Paris, 1 March 1981.

beginning of women's movements – in France since 1970 where it was 'resolved' by the stifling of the 'political lesbian' current.[1]

Since last year, while one part of the women's movement (in contradiction with their own analysis which posits two antagonistic sex-classes) chose what could be called a 'reformist' struggle in relation to the class of men, another part has begun to push the logic of radical feminism to its conclusion, and identifies with a lesbian political analysis which considers the *class of men* to be the main enemy. What is therefore at stake is an overall strategy in which the question of choice of lifestyle – in a movement which states that the personal is political – has been the revealing factor.

No. 7 of *QF* (February 1980) had reopened the lesbianism/heterosexuality debate by publishing two articles: one, by Monique Wittig ('Straight Thinking') denounced the existence of a heterosexual logic which is oppressive for all women. The other article, by E. de Lesseps ('Heterosexuality and feminism'), raised the question of feminist politics and commitment and answered it by saying: you *can* be feminist and heterosexual (in spite of 'contradictions'). The first article didn't talk at all about heterosexual feminists; the second, however, talked of lesbians as if they were objects, stating (instead of leaving lesbians to make their own statements) that they hadn't 'chosen' their 'sexuality', that their lifestyle was not therefore one of political commitment, hereby reducing all lesbian political statements to a corporatist defence of 'sexual interests'.

On 14 March 1980, during a movement-wide meeting about this issue of *QF*, a heated discussion began. Lesbians who belonged to *different groups* (and not just the Jussieu group): first, posed that heterosexuality seemed to them to be a choice that was antagonistic to feminist commitment and at any rate was dangerous to claim as terrain for individual struggle; and second opposed the reductive nature of a dominant discourse which reduces homosexuality to nothing more than an inevitability caused by psychological determinism. What is important is that a homosexual woman has a *de facto* behaviour which objectively opposes the oppressor, even if she is unaware of it, even if she sees her own experience as 'impelled by an urge', as 'different', even as 'abnormal'.

This statement of position by lesbians – who formed a united front by claiming that lesbianism is a political position and not a different 'sexuality' – came *after* certain strategic conflicts had already broken out within the movement, in particular during the preparations of 8 March (International Women's Day). With the purpose of opposing *Psych et Po*, who by appropriating the logo MLF had made concrete their openly declared antifeminism, certain radical feminists sought to join up with the *Co-ordination des groupes femmes* (Women's groups inside the workplace and in different neighbourhoods) whom they had in fact fought for years over their strategic ambiguity.[2] The alliance against *Psych et Po* with this Co-ordination, still imbued with a certain 'Marxist' logic from the 'class struggle' current (bourgeoisie/proletariat), seemed to a number of lesbians to be dangerous for our radicalism. During the preparations for 8 March, subversive slogans against, for instance, the family (heterosexual institution *par excellence*), were rejected and only the expression 'struggle against patriarchy' was accepted, hiding real oppositions by its vagueness.

In the interests of unity the agreed decision over March 8 was that each group would march under its own banner with the Co-ordination at the head. But when they saw *Psych et Po* force their way to the head of the march without any intervention from the Co-ordination, lesbians from the Jussieu group, the North Paris suburbs group among others and members of the 1000 currents group rejected a united sheep-like submission: they went to the head of the march and kicked *Psych et Po* out of the esplanade where the demonstration was going to end and we were all going to meet.

The question of the feminist movement's strategy also came up during specific actions (against rape, against violence) and was shown to be closely linked to the lesbianism/heterosexuality conflict.

The terms of this debate were very clearly expressed on 6 June 1980 during a second meeting about no. 7 *QF*, which focused on the overview of 'ten years of feminism'. The question seemed to be the following: could understanding of the movement's history help us define strategies for our struggle, given the current 'repressive political conditions' (Law and Order bills, Afghanistan, Third World War?) Some women said that, because of these conditions, it was important to become involved again in 'general struggles' speaking and acting as feminists. Lesbians condemned the fact that by posing the problems in these terms, the generality of the women's liberation struggle was denied, and that it was killing radical feminism by hiding the fact that the oppression of the class of women by the class of men was present in all oppressions. It is by devoting all our energies to our liberation that we could contribute most effectively to the transformation of social relations as a whole.

The question of lesbian participation in feminism ten years ago, and the stifling of a political lesbian current were also raised; several participants wanted old conflicts, which had been silenced and which now seemed to be coming out again, to be clarified. The debate was very stormy and ended with women exchanging insults: a 'bisexual' feminist called a lesbian a 'bloke' and was called 'a collaborator' in return, by a lesbian (from the Jussieu group) – an insult typical of the dominant system on the one side (a woman who escapes from men and speaks with a certain degree of violence sees herself called a 'bloke' yet again), but an internal political accusation on the other ('collabo'). There is no equivalence between these two positions any more than there is between the privileged status that heterosexual women enjoy in relation to lesbians, and the social repression that lesbians are subjected to every day. Following that event, a rumour began to circulate against 'radical lesbians' identifying them with a 'Jussieu – terrorist – elitist – bolshevik line' (and more of the same).

During the lesbian meeting in Paris on 21–2 June 1980 (organized by the Jussieu group), the writing was (literally) on the walls, and – to remind us that we are in a state of war of the sexes and that we have real commitments to make – lesbians (not from the Jussieu group) pasted up posters. The following quotes are taken from some of the posters.

A woman who loves her oppressor, is oppressed. A 'Feminist' who loves her oppressor is a collaborator.

In the war of the sexes, hetero-feminism is class collaboration.

Apologetic dykes, don't be ashamed of your sexuality. That's not what it's about.

Homosexual women, don't be ashamed of your lesbianism. That's what it's about.

Hetero-'Feminists' – kapos for patriarchy.

Hetero-'feminism' divides the class of women. Apologetic lesbianism betrays it.

Texts, written by the Jussieu group of lesbians, were suggested as subject for discussion, but the homosexual feminists[3] present only wanted to talk about what was on the walls, which was obviously not explanatory in content. Also, the only statements that were discussed were those that addressed 'poor old heteros' and not those directed to homosexual women themselves about the political assertion of their lesbianism. Out of this meeting came the caricature: hetero = collabo.

During (and together with) these events, from March to June, a political opposition which until then had been unspoken came out within the QF collective. The attack began in June and was directed against the only woman in the group who asserted that she was a political lesbian (and who participated in the Jussieu group). She was called on to withdraw her insults (which she hadn't made), to 'denounce' 'her' position (which nobody let her explain), and she was threatened with either leaving the collective, because it was judged illogical on her part to continue to work with heterosexuals, or, if she refused, to force the heterosexual woman in the collective who considered herself 'insulted' to resign. The split quickly developed into two sub-groups: on the one hand, of two women who rejected political lesbianism for its 'lack of courtesy' and its 'rudeness'; on the other, of three women who had either participated in lesbian groups or were interested in a kind of thinking that can't be summed up by a slogan and who, in declaring their solidarity with this lesbian, showed their position of lesbianism. (We knew that the political split was not a question of the defence of 'sexual interests' because there were heterosexuals and homosexuals in both camps.) The schism was a fundamental one, and affected the collective as it affects the movement.

In the (November 1977) editorial, we had set out a theoretical analysis of the relations of oppression between the sexes but we hadn't (yet) begun thinking about strategies for our struggle.

We had spoken of the need to suppress hierarchy, to denounce the ideology of Difference which made oppression something to do with Nature. But how are the power relations to which women are subjected made concrete except via the constraint of living with the oppressor, depending on him objectively, which leads to the constraint of heterosexuality? What strategy can be used against sex-classes: is it 'struggling with' the class of men ('reformist' strategy) or considering them absolutely as an enemy class ('radical' strategy)?

We had said that oppression did not sum up our entire being, and that the contradictions of our social system allowed us to be critical, to have a feminist perspective. By that we were talking about the possibility of ideological resistance, but we didn't go as far as the concrete forms – the practical forms – that this resistance to oppression could take. We had, among other things, not talked about the existence and the role of lesbians – those women who reject the oppressor, whose emotional life is exclusively directed towards women, who reject traditional 'femininity'

– those ways of resisting heterosexual power without which feminism could not have existed and could not go on existing.

Radical lesbianism is not a 'sexual preference' or only 'liking to live with women'. It is a decisive political choice which is implicit in the analysis of sex-class relations based on exploitation and oppression and which have antagonistic interests. Lesbian political commitment is different from the feminism of 'homosexuals' or 'heterosexuals' because we choose to use the margins of freedom, of manoeuvre, that the patriarchal system leaves us, to fight it at its roots: the power of sex Difference. This is to say that in theoretical terms, we are trying to articulate the *determinism* of oppression and the *resistance* to oppression.

The lesbian choice is *mobilization*, in a visible collective movement, and the transfer of all our creative powers, both intellectual and emotional, to women, because we all have the same class interests. Far from wanting to carve out spaces for ourselves in a hetero-patriarchal society which objectifies, oppresses and kills women, we want to fight the mechanisms of its power.

The lesbian choice is *awareness* that male violence against women is at work everywhere, especially in 'private' life, with its traps of emotional attachment or heterosexual 'desire'. It is decision turned *into act* to use certain social conditions which allow us to reject the material and psychological privileges that men give to those women who are still under the illusion that, in certain exchanges with the enemy, they can escape their own oppression as women. Heterosexual power – which dispenses these privileges – is, in our view, a fundamental strategy of patriarchy, which forces women to depend on those who are objectively their oppressors. In this sense, political subversion means that we must attack heterosexual norms at their roots, criticize the structure of heterosexuality, and not patch it up.

The – theoretical and strategic – opposition between radical lesbians, on the one hand, and feminists who claim that heterosexuality is an area of struggle on the other, has finally turned against lesbians: because they talked about 'complicity', about 'class collaboration', radical lesbians have been accused of 'inflicting guilt' on radical feminists and of 'forcing' them either to make radical changes in their private lives, or to 'give up' the feminist struggle. As if it wasn't the objective power of men over women that 'forces' certain women to flee from radicalism, and certain women to flee from the movement!

We say that heterosexuality is not a simple question of a predetermined 'sexual orientation' any more than homosexuality is. Saying that one is 'not able to desire women', is remaining within the logic of servicing men's interests; it is reinforcing one's own oppression. For women caught in heterosexuality and who want to get out of the contradictions that that brings as feminists, only the open assertion of the existence, the possibility and the political meaning of lesbianism can help them get away from heterosexuality.

A political position that attacks a norm which is oppressive for all women (hetero-power) is subversive, although it may be violent in its questioning of feminists (feminism is itself violent for non-feminist women). On the other hand, a discourse which reassures this norm – in spite of its nuances and contradictions – reinforces the legitimacy of the norm, the legitimacy of the power of men over women, and can only work against their liberation. And this discourse turns against those women, lesbians, who declare that they are irreducible and irreconcilable enemies of the class of oppressors. It is in defence of a strategy and a theory that can be called 'heterofeminist' – legitimation of the norm – that feminists have attacked lesbians, and it is to 'support' these positions that homosexual women have broken their solidarity with radical lesbians.

It is not lesbians who have 'divided' the movement or who have 'killed' *Questions Féministes*. It is the power of the class of men which has – once again – divided us.

Notes and references

1   Other women deny that there was any 'stifling' of lesbianism in the MLF.
2   The relationship between radical feminism and the neighbourhood groups, which were mostly organized by 'class struggle convert' feminists was often difficult with disagreements over the relationship of the MLF to the united left, and the role of men in feminism. See Part One.
3   'Homosexual feminists' refers to lesbians in the women's movement who are not political lesbians.

Extract from radical lesbian tract*

Collective for a lesbian front

We claim as ours the political identity of lesbian as we are no longer satisfied with that of feminist, because we want to express clearly who is the enemy and with whom we are in solidarity. If the concept of feminism contains the idea of women's oppression and of struggle, the notion of lesbianism posits the basis of this oppression (heterosociality) and a strategy of resistance and struggle (radical break with the class of oppressors). Just as we believed in calling ourselves feminists because of the historical content of this notion, because we wanted to reassert our solidarity with all the women resisters of the past who cleared the path for us, so we believe in calling ourselves lesbians to affirm our community with all those resisters – 'dykes', 'homosexual women' – who show by their lives that it is impossible for them to submit in their daily lives to the private power relations between men and women. This impossibility is not due to a psychological insufficiency, an emotional impotence, a fatal flaw or a disaster – even if it is experienced as such by individual women – it constitutes, objectively, a *subversive political practice*: sketchy if it remains isolated and individual, aggressive if it becomes a collective consciousness.

This practice is often unconsciously experienced as revolt, which doesn't mean it has no impact: it is no accident that the first feminists, even before the assertion of political lesbianism, were called lesbians, because oppressors knew full well that all lesbians were fighting them, in a political strategy. We demand the systematization of this practice. We say that: first, lesbianism is the rejection of the power relation that men impose on women, and is the acting upon this rejection in real life, at the level of private appropriation (domestic, family, sexual, emotional) and of collective appropriation (rejection of 'femininity', the submission demanded

*7–8 March 1981.

of women in the street, at work. Second, we say that this rejection is aimed at an institution that is oppressive for all women and not at a 'desire', an 'impulse', a 'sexuality' or against biological, as opposed to social, man. Like all things, heterosexuality is historical and social: it is the most effective means that the class of men has used to constrain the class of women to submit, concretely, to the relations of oppression, to think of them as inevitable and to seek them out as terrain for self-affirmation.

This rejection is radical because it is in no sense conciliatory or compromising about power relations: lesbianism is a subversive movement of solidarity because it includes 'private' communication between women, which is in actual opposition to the division that heteropower introduces between women, exchange objects for men to exchange and, as such, rivals.

For us, the revolution does not consist of waiting for the Great Day but of setting up means of resistance *now*. Which is why we say that our strategy must be made concrete *in our lives* in the clearest, most radical way possible.

We politically assert our lesbianism – which is in our political analyses, our way of life, our identity, the tactics and the networks we have set up so that we don't submit to power relations – because this assertion is doubly essential:

First, it constitutes an alternative political struggle and an alternative life for women who want to break with all circuits of dependence on men. We are in solidarity with the struggles in which they are engaged which will enable them to escape, completely (without any compromise) in their material lives, in their identity, in their thinking, in their emotional lives, in their bodies, from men's 'protection', from men's gaze, from men's 'desire'. But we are not in solidarity with feminists who claim heterosexuality as a 'terrain for struggle' because they are defending a collaborationist, reformist strategy with the class of oppressors; the strategy of heterofeminism. We would agree that it is a 'strategy like others' if it didn't turn against us and against the majority of women: it states that men are not all oppressors only and nothing else, so that some of them are spared, 'new men'; it legitimates and defends that which is socially dominant and oppressive: heterosexual norms, hetero-power. Heterofeminism is a useless blow against the class of men, but is a dagger in the back of lesbians and therefore of the whole class of women.

Second, this assertion of lesbianism is indispensable for isolated lesbians, who think that they're abnormal and are restricted to living with guilt, fear, in the ghetto; indispensable, so that they can recognize in their way of life a certain political resistance and find this strength to become a visible, collective movement which acknowledges itself for what it really is: subversion.

Radical lesbians, lesbian feminists, lesbianists, we are trying to say out loud who the enemy is, how we are oppressed and how we can respond. While we may disagree about our Utopias, about the status of our theoretical work, about our tactics for our struggle, we are nevertheless in agreement about creating a lesbian front which asserts our position as radically subversive.

Heteroppression*

Icamiaba

Oppression, resistance, determination, struggle not to live as 'oppressed people', political spaces allowing us to resist, to create alternative lifestyles and to destroy the hetero-patriarchal system. Words, questions, choices – about our lives!

The total refusal to accept *oppression* as 'natural', *non-resistance* as 'natural', *collaboration* as 'natural'. We don't believe in a 'bright tomorrow', but in our ways of resisting and of creating ways in which we can live in a society which is stifling us; in a society where the word 'life' doesn't mean anything; in a society which we find repulsive and in which we feel uneasy and uncomfortable. Well, what can you expect. We're just maladjusted, we haven't internalized the whole thing, we have taken apart, and continue to take apart, every day, the mechanisms and ideology of hetero-patriarchal power which oppresses us. We do this collectively: it is only in this way that we can live, that we can give meaning to the word 'life'.

We exist because we believe that we can choose, create and destroy. The age-old oppression, which lies in wait for us at our birth, can be rejected by a never-ending daily struggle against a system based on the power of one class: men.

Heteropower, power of 'difference', positing 'difference' which means positing *complementarity*, in the name of 'nature' ('mother of all evil'), and now in the name of 'sexuality', in the name of 'love'.

We believe that heterosexuality is socially constructed, that it is one of the pillars of patriarchy, that it is not a 'moral' norm but a political strategy which makes it possible to keep a system going, to perpetuate it, hide its contradictions, mask the oppressors and above all *divide* us 'in the name of

---

*From *Nouvelles Questions Féministes*, no. 1, March 1981; published as part of the debate on radical lesbianism and representing the opposite point of view from the NQF collective.

love', make us renounce our class allegiance, make us even turn against our own interests.

'In the name of love'! The kindly look which acknowledges our existence; their codes; the sweetness of conformity, security and comfort. In the name of oppression, accept that world, theirs, the trap, the making-do, the compromise, gratitude, submission, life. But what kind of life?

'You're killing yourselves', they said. Fear of loss, fear of isolation, fear of walking together – us, not future generations! Fear of our own revolt, of violence, of our political positions with which we can destroy the 'hetero-patriarchal system' in our heads and in society, and where we can create our own spaces, where life is possible.

What has lesbians' contribution to feminism been over the past ten years? It was lesbians who began the women's movement, lesbians who kept up the pressure so that our small groups didn't simply become places for sorting out our relationships with men; it was lesbians who most emphatically insisted on keeping the MLF women-only (both in terms of male presence and in terms of the content of our discussions and actions).

Lesbians were involved in the struggle for abortion, against rape, for control of our bodies. Lesbians were so visible because of their refusal to look like 'women', to look 'feminine', because they denounced men as a class and denounced relationships with them, founded on power based on the appropriation of women's bodies. All feminists (even heteros) were called lesbians. In this man's world, the term 'lesbian' represents the non-appropriated, the enemy, rivals, 'abnormal women' (this reassures them) . . . in fact, it represents *danger* for a hetero-patriarchal society.

But in spite of the strong presence of lesbians in the MLF, groups of lesbians meeting separately have been uncommon. We called ourselves homosexuals rather than lesbians, implying that lesbianism is a form of different sexuality rather than a political position of struggle against patriarchy, and thereby considering women's heterosexuality as a kind of sexuality and not as the basic power strategy of the class of men.

Feminism has not exposed how heterosexuality is a strategy of patriarchal power exercised against women; how it *isn't* a form of sexuality; how it is in contradiction with the interests of the class of women.

Feminism cannot advance theoretically unless it confronts these problems: theory can only be elaborated from a basis of political practice. This is why we say that lesbianism is the future of feminism.

The first insult addressed to lesbians is that of 'not being women'. This phrase haunts and hurts us. We experience it as aggression against us.

We know, today, what the word 'woman' means, how it refers to the image of women that patriarchy imposes on us in order to oppress us more (and justifying it by saying that we are different); how the term refers to the 'other', man, and to the right of appropriating women that their society gives them.

No. We are not women, we're lesbians. We aren't 'homosexuals', we don't 'love women', we don't 'make love with women': we choose to live our lives together, without differences, without power, in solidarity with our own class, rejecting the oppressive public/private distinction, and aware that our movement undermines the oppressive system against which we are engaged in a struggle to the death.

Radical/lie natural/lie*[1]

On the difference between a lesbian and a homosexual woman

Catherine Deudon

When a man has just called you a filthy homosexual, just tell him – to see what happens – that, no, you are a distinguished lesbian, and see if he can tell the political difference. Apart from the fact that he won't find you any more distinguished (or political), he will also wonder if you're not just a little crazy. There is nothing that makes a political distinction possible between the words 'lesbian' and 'homosexual', giving the former a greater subversive character than the latter. The word 'lesbian' is in no sense a political concept; all it is is a synonym for a 'female homosexual', attached to the poetess Sappho, born on Lesbos, nothing more. On the other hand, whether you are 'homo' or 'hetero', tell him you're a feminist. Then, he will realize so clearly that you are declaring political war (with a real, political word) that he will do his utmost to repress it. And if this real political word makes him furiously angry, it is precisely because it means that what puts you in opposition to him can't be explained purely by your homosexuality, nor by you as an individual. The word 'feminism' points to the fact that what opposes you to each other as individuals is linked to a question of sex-class opposition. As this is precisely what he will not understand, he reassures himself by reducing it to the status of a specific neurosis. A feminist movement consisting only of homosexual women – now that would reassure him! He would find the categories he knows – of Nature (with Real Women, who love men) and Anti-Nature, (with these failed, bad women, who hate men). If all women, hetero and homo, were feminists (and feminist means for all women), he would get confused. It would give him nightmares.

If *all* of us are involved in feminism their myths crumble; both the myth of the Real Woman and that of the failed, damned anti-nature woman (that

*From *La Revue d'en Face*, no. 9/10, 1981.

is, the double, the shady repressed side of the Real Woman. Anti-Nature has never meant against the naturalist ideology as explanation of social relations. It rather confirms this ideology, by opposing a bad-nature to the good one).

Are all feminists lesbians, or not? He doesn't know any more, poor thing, and neither do we. Who used to be hetero will be homo tomorrow . . . and vice versa (although this is not so common at the moment). This is what radicalism is, that's all, it doesn't belong to any one group exclusive.

However, some homosexual women, (not all of them) sporadically claim as theirs a radically differentiating label, whose logical conclusion is 'lesbian separatism'. The result of this ideology (of ideological separatism, not strategic separatism, like the MLF's segregation) is the aspiration to the Land of the Chosen women: the Lesbian Nation, a larger-scale version of the ghetto – which leaves patriarchy intact. The Lesbian Nation is in fundamental agreement with the Patriarchal Nation over the notion of 'Woman' (and the opposite concept of 'the lesbian as non-Woman').

What is more, 'lesbian' is the only concept I know that goes beyond sex categories (woman and man) because the subject (the lesbian) is not, in economic, political and ideological terms, a woman (Monique Wittig, *Questions Féministes*, no.7).

(She is raped, why? She is underpaid, why? She is kept silent, why – unless it is because she is a woman whose class is dominated by the class of men? And on top of that, she is discriminated against inside her own class of women for her homosexuality.)

In agreement with the Patriarchal Nation, then, over the concept of 'Woman' and 'Non-Woman/lesbian', the population of the Chosen in the Lesbian Nation will quarrel with equal chauvinism over the appropriation of women! ('One aspect of lesbian oppression consists in the fact that women are out of our reach, because women belong to men', M. Wittig.)

Resolutely, radically feminist, I believe in the destruction of sex categories (expanded by the same M. Wittig in her article 'One is Not Born a Woman') and I believe thereby, as a logical consequence, in the destruction of categories of sexual practices.

This is why, although I am homosexual, I have no desire for this chauvinist, sexist, Lesbian Nation, which is merely an avatar of the 'elsewhere' of a sectarian sect like *Psychanalyse et Politique*, making the 'symbolic revolution' and women's 'erotic independence' on the backs of women.

We used to have to be heterosexual to be a Real Woman, the Woman of the patriarchal myth (and now the lesbian myth).

Must we now be obliged to be lesbian to be a Real Non-woman, the Non-woman of the radical lesbian myth!

In short, we have understood, this radicalism is nothing more than a reversal which makes us find nature in the Lesbian Anti-Nature, Woman in the Non-woman . . . and pariahs (previously homosexual) in heterosexual women.

Let us not lose our feminism, and let us stay, without shame, homosexual feminists (not lesbianists), that is, situated in the class of women and struggling with this class against women's oppression, to which is added (not removed) my specific oppression as a homosexual.

This ideology of Radical Anti-Nature, which claims, like *Psych et Po*, to have conquered oppression is also, of course, another incarnation of the ideology of Difference (replaced by the concept of 'more radical' and by that of 'separate/separatist'). It slides from categories of sex to those of sexual practices. It is hardly coincidence that they share an immediately obvious implicit anti-feminism, by the way that 'feminism' is replaced by 'lesbianism'. This conjuring trick is saying that 'lesbianism' means 'feminism', only more radical!

If communities of homosexual women are formed and break up today, without too many worries about repression, it is thanks to the MLF, to its different changing forms of socialization, to its struggles, writings, creations relating to both hetero – and homosexuality.

Homosexuality since the movement, inside, with (and even outside but thanks to) the movement is not the same as homosexuality before the movement. The same applies to heterosexuality. The struggle against the oppression and repression of homosexuality is undoubtedly one of the movement's essential tasks. On condition that is does not exclude others. On condition that it is defined as feminist, that. is, a struggle against sex categories and thereby the categories of sexual practices linked to them. In other words, a struggle of feminist homosexuals and not of lesbianists; in solidarity with lesbians but not separatist; radical but not *more* radical; anti-naturalist and therefore anti-anti-naturalist; anti-feminine and therefore anti-masculine; anti-Woman and therefore for women.

Notes and references

1   In correspondence (October 1985), Catherine Deudon pointed out that she had shared many of Monique Wittig's ideas before her QF articles, and that she holds Wittig in great esteem. She also adds that she thinks that the violence of feeling expressed during the radical feminist/political lesbian split in 1981 would be out of place now.

Hating masculinity not men*[1]

Marie-Jo Dhavernas

Among the MLF's most important tasks to my mind, is, the attempt to pick up the ways in which we reproduce the models – both theoretical and practical – given to us by patriarchal society (everyone knows that the oppressed have always tended to imitate their masters). This is why I would like first to show how the theory known as 'radical lesbianism' – and which we often call 'separatist' – fits into traditional modes of thought rather than it destroying them, and second, to discuss its paradoxes.

This theory originates with the critique of the ideology of difference, a critique with which we can all agree – except those plunged into the delights of 'neo-femininity' – 'traitors' and 'collaborators'. Unless one is talking in terms of a moral abstraction, the first question we must ask is whether separatism is the best, or the only, way of struggling against the ideology of difference and the patriarchal system it underpins.

We should note first of all that if lesbianism (and more generally homosexuality in both sexes) upsets the notion of *complementarity* of the sexes, it does not do much against the notion of *difference*, which incorporates complementarity but is not reducible to it. Racists see Blacks, Arabs, Asians, etc., as different from whites, but not as particularly complementary to them. This is not without significance – on the contrary – because the myth of complementarity is the specific form that the racist ideology of (natural) difference adopts where relations between the sexes are concerned, at least in our society. It is a myth perpetuated by innumerable dichotomies expressed in terms of sexuality. From this point of view, it is clear that lesbianism is a vital issue, and one that all feminists must confront.

Yet does it necessarily follow that radical lesbianism (not to be confused with simple homosexual practice) is both essential to, and sufficient for, the destruction of patriarchy? Monique Wittig seems to think that it is:

*From *La Revue d'en Face*, no. 9/10, 1981.

'lesbian' is the only concept I know that goes beyond sex categories (woman and man), because the subject (lesbian) is not, in economic, political or ideological terms, a woman. For in fact, what makes a woman is a particular social relationship to a man, which we have called 'servage' – a relationship which implies personal and physical obligations as well as economic obligations . . . a relationship from which lesbians escape by refusing to become or to stay heterosexual.

This quotation reveals clearly both the illusory nature of separatism and the way in which it remains trapped within patriarchal discourse.

The belief that refusing all contact with men is enough to make a woman a 'non-woman', as Wittig says, is not only an illusion but is also in contradiction with the notion of sex-class. As long as there is a system which is founded on two totally distinct 'sex-classes', it will be impossible to step out of the class in which one was born, as society will continue to treat those who see themselves as 'escapees' in exactly the same way as the others. Are lesbians safe from rape? From men's attempts to pick them up? From discrimination at work? From sexist insults? No, of course not. Maybe they are less exposed to them, but as long as they live in a patriarchal society, 'non-women' or not, they will be subjected to the same oppression as all women.

In the passage quoted above, M. Wittig cheerfully mixes together paradigm and reality. Her analysis of the duties of 'servage' no longer applies in legal terms, and does not express women's reality in France today – and even less that of *feminist* heterosexuals. Part of her description applies, of course, in a 'normal' situation, but what percentage of women actually live in a 'normal' situation? Apart from its contemptuous attitude to heterosexual women, presumed to consent to such slavery, all that this analysis expresses is patriarchy's ideal status for women, not the actual experience of a growing number of women.

If heterosexual relations are still dominated by phallocratic behaviour, it is certainly not at the level of this private 'appropriation' which is tending to disappear among the young, as the differentiation between sex roles becomes blurred – including in those milieux relatively unaffected by feminism. This blurring happens in behaviour, attitudes, reactions, talking, guilt infliction and in all these ways of being on which little boys and little girls have been modelled.

As for the private appropriation described by M. Wittig, you don't have to be a lesbian to escape it. It is true that egalitarian relationships between a woman and a man require constant expenditure of energy, constant vigilance and a never-ending struggle against cultural inertia. It is also true that this struggle is all the harder to engage in, as it has such great emotional investment. This is not, as the radical lesbians think, purely sentimental dependence, but is active, the construction and deconstruction of complex and ambivalent relationships; it does eat up energy – but my energy belongs to me, not to women any more than to men, not even to the movement, to which I have never sworn an oath of allegiance. Heterosexuality, we are told in one radical lesbian text, 'depoliticizes the men/women antagonism, by individualizing and "humanizing" relations of oppression'. Funny way to conceive of our old slogan 'the personal is political' (formally reasserted by the separatists), when, from this perspective, it ought to read 'there is no personal, only political'. The radical lesbians reduce the personal to the political in the same way as patriarchy reduces the political to the personal, or denies the emotional dimension of the political. Feminists, on the contrary, affirm that the emotional and the political interact and affect each other, but neither can be reduced to the other.

The fact that all men, because of their sex, are in the position of oppressor does not mean that all male individuals *are nothing but oppressor* – any more than we are not *nothing but oppressed*. (If this were the case, we wouldn't even be able to fight.) It is because oppression *fails* to make us purely oppressors or purely oppressed that liberation is conceivable: and it is clearly more useful to pick out the system's faults than to inflate its victories.

The very notion of 'non-women' implies that one may leave one's 'sex-class'; but then if a woman can evade her status as oppressed by stopping all contact with men (an idea which puts Carmelite nuns at the forefront of the feminist struggle – if only the Pope knew!), then, following the same logic, a man should be able to escape his status as oppressor by stopping all contact with women.

How can the positing of 'non-women' be reconciled with the affirmation that 'all men are rapists, all men are men'? What is this difference between the two sexes that makes a woman who is not 'appropriated' no longer a woman, while a man who does not 'appropriate' a woman remains a man? A choice must be made: either 'sex-classes' are such a rigid category that one cannot step outside until the last misogynist has been hung with the intestines of the last sexist, in which case it is true that 'all men are rapists, all men are men', but in this case, there would be no such thing as a feminist, let alone a 'non-woman'. Or else it is possible to step outside one's 'sex-class' and there are indeed 'non-women'. But then there would also be, at least hypothetically, 'non-men' (who are therefore not oppressors), with whom relations cannot be of oppressed to oppressor and therefore not of collaboration – which would paradoxically reintroduce heterosexuality with these non-men, heterosociality and even possibly cast doubts on the women-only nature of the movement.

On the other hand, it could be that things are not so simple. There are different degrees of oppression; women and men objectively belong to their respective 'sex-class' without being limited to it; and behaviour, actions, words are more important at the level of each individual than social and biological adherence to a sex; and women can be more and more feminist, and men can be less and less sexist, but not all at the same time and not all at the same rhythm.

This is the only way of seeing things that allows me to conceive of liberation: for I can hardly imagine that a *coup d'état* or a violent revolution, even geographical partition (as if these solutions weren't crazy in the first place) could suddenly bring an end to sexist ideology and its internalization by women and men.

This clearly does not bring the movement's women-only policy into question (for even if there did exist any totally non-sexist men, they would still not share our female condition); nor does it doubt that today, whether they like it or not, all men benefit from patriarchy but suggests that they are not necessarily proponents of oppression nor propagandists of male chauvinism.

Some women say: you're deluding yourselves. Men are incapable of change, because patriarchy is in their interests. OK, but what interests? An 'objective' material interest and a social and psychological interest, which is a bit pathetic. But why give sexual oppression a status we deny other oppressions? I am western and socially privileged; I have 'objective' interests (as do many of us) in maintaining the oppression and exploitation of the Third World and the proletariat, from whom I derive benefits whether I like it or not. However, I am engaged in a struggle against imperialism, and for an egalitarian, self-managing society. Rather than feeling myself to be in a fanciful way 'superior', by nature, I prefer, for the price of a few material advantages and a bit of prestige, to live in a world of fully-developed human beings, equal and free. This is *also* in my interest, and I regard it more highly than the cowlike satisfaction of cheap elitism, which is as much of a trap as it is de-humanizing. I therefore do not see by which quirk of fate men should be different from me in this, *by definition,* and why they shouldn't end up – even if it is a particularly long and diffi-cult process – by realizing this interest, by becoming anti-sexist for the same reasons which make me an anti-racist. (And if they don't, we will never have a post-patriarchal society.) I know that what I have just written exposes me to accusations of complacency or self-indulgence. I am, how-ever, no less of a man-hater than the next woman; but my man-hating is directed at 'masculinity' and not at men, or rather at men according to the degree of their masculinity. That is, I take into account what they are socially. (At least one advantage of 'heterosociality' is to allow us to see that our ten-year struggle has already had some effect.) The fact that there is continuity between the slightest discrimination and the most extreme servitude does not mean that everything has equal weight. To indulge in verbal inflation which equates flirtation with rape, and fantasy with the act, is to make rape more anodyne, is to give arguments to men who distance themselves from their sexist practices by blaming the system, and who shrug off guilt as active authors of oppression by assigning it to the role they are given in patriarchal society. If they are called rapists when they have never raped anyone, why should they not do so? It's not their fault, 'it's the system', it's sexual alienation, it's their education, etc. We know these arguments only too well. But the only way to get them to change is to make them see their personal responsibility in the perpetra-tion of oppression, to remove all ideological and material escape routes. To amalgamate everything would go against this consciousness which we must constantly try to provoke.

Radical lesbians seem to forget that the end of oppression implies that either men are exterminated (which is unrealistic, even if it were desir-able), or that they change completely. And feminism involves *all* the ways to achieve this goal. Excluding them from our struggle and from our space is one of these ways. It has already begun to show its effectiveness, notably by forcing a certain number of them to admit that it wasn't only the 'system' which was oppressing us, but also them, on a personal level, as agents of this system: and then by teaching them to see things relatively, destroying the base of their complacency.

Ceasing all contact with men is a strategy whose value I don't doubt. But confronting them every day, constantly showing them the ways in which they are oppressive, changing power relations by conquering our freedom not only apart from them but in front of them, forcing them more and more to recognize that women are people and not objects, destroying their interest in maintaining their privileges by making sure that they receive more injuries than advantages from them – this is not 'collaboration', it is a daily struggle, even if this struggle is permeated by emotions (and all struggles are, I think, in a thousand ways). It is the heterosexual, hetero-social form of the feminist struggle. We have the right not to like it. And I still have not seen how, in separatist texts, lesbianism is adequate in itself to uproot the phallocratic mentality without which patriarchy could not be sustained.

'We don't like men', writes Monique. Neither do we: we like individual men. 'We don't like women', adds Icamiaba. Neither do we: we like individual women. Our solidarity doesn't need to be based on love, but, equally, our love doesn't have to be based on solidarity. We have solidarity with a 'sex-class' but we *love* individual people. Women, says Monique, 'learn how to betray their class for the benefit of others', to 'cut themselves off from the Same, and betray them'.

The Same? What Same? For me, everyone is an other, men and women. Nothing inspires me with more horror than this fusing of female identity, in which, although starting from different premises, radical lesbians and the praisers of 'neo-femininity' come together. If I found all women identical, in what way would they interest me? I don't need to look at myself in a mirror. Excessive similarity is as abhorrent as total 'otherness'. What I like in women, as in men, is the play of similarity and difference, what resembles me and what doesn't. To be identical is to disappear, and women have suffered only too much from this imposed and internalized disappearance of their individuality for the sake of their sexual group. The difference is not between men and women, but between 4000 million human individuals.

Radical lesbians write that patriarchy separates us, that 'heteroppression radically divides women'. But to speak of patriarchy dividing women without saying that it is also patriarchy that unites us, and to say that lesbianism is the 'root' of feminism, supposes an adherence – not necessarily conscious – to the belief that poses a unity between women independently of patriarchy, outside or before it: which, in an oblique way, brings us back to the question of 'difference'. If there is no (natural) difference between the sexes, all we have in common is our oppression and our internalization of this oppression. We are not *the same*, we are only in *the same situation*. As for what divides us – it is not heterosexuality, which in no sense prevents us from struggling together, but is rather the attempt to separate out the 'non-women' from the 'women'.

I don't want to be defined by my 'choice of object' any more than by my biological status. I'm a heterosexual? You're the one who says so. I myself do not see myself in any category and each of my relationships has its own character.

What is this fantasy of homogeneity which makes some women propose a foolish femin-idiotism with goals of revenge rather than subversion ('betrayal') to the point that they *use* patriarchal definitions/categories instead of destroying them; which pushes others to suggest that there is one kind of women's sexual pleasure, defined by their own preferences, and which exercises a terrorism to the point that it becomes the *only* viable kind? I don't want to mask where separatism and neo-femininity differ, but it is also time to see what they have in common.

'Nature's other', a discussion in *Sorcières* between F. Clédat, X. Gauthier, L. Irigaray and A.M. de Vilaine[2] is very enlightening on this point. Irigaray states 'the feminine element in men is not the same as the feminine element in women, nor the masculine in women the same as the masculine in men'; there is therefore supposedly a masculine essence and a feminine essence, existing outside men and women but incarnated by them. Nothing could at first appear more in opposition to this ethereal idealism than the laborious positions of radical lesbianism; it is only the result which is the same – the imposition of norms. Irigaray writes:

Bisexuality, recently become very fashionable, seems to me to be full of traps. . . . When we deny our difference in order to achieve equality, are we not accomplices? In fact, are we not accomplices in the ascent of Western masculine imperialism? Rejecting women's oppression is not the same thing as rejecting our bodies, our sexuality, our Imaginary, our language . . . but it means that we must discover them and speak them, affirm their value. Does fighting racism mean rejecting your race?

The similarity of language in the two discourses can hardly be coincidental. For the first, I betray my class, for the second, I deny my sex. For the first, I am a collaborator, for the second, I am an accomplice. Both of them deny *my* desire.

Our bodies, our sexuality, our Imaginary, our language? Where? I have my own body, and the fact that it is anatomically the same as the bodies of other women does not mean that it has the same desires, the same pleasures. I have my own sexuality and I will never know whether it is the same as my neighbour's. I have my own Imaginary, which has very little in common with what is expressed in *Sorcières*. I have my own language, which is neither Wittig's nor Irigaray's. You're right, 'mother earth' is not my thing. According to *Sorcières*, I am a renegade – have I fallen from the grace of my female sexuality? Should I be called an 'a-sexid'? I am neither a woman nor a non-woman; I am even beginning to wonder if I exist.

The radical lesbians assert that their homosexuality is a 'political choice'. Unusual idea, which, applied to anything else would seem ludicrous: usually a desire would lead to making a choice. Hard to believe that you just need to be a feminist to reverse cause and effect and have choice arouse desire.

I accept, of course, that desires can change because of ideological changes, which we can call 'choices' out of convenience. But in that case, how can the internalization of patriarchal values be explained? If women have submitted to oppression for so long, it is surely because they haven't really been free.

It is true that there are situations, possibilities and new ideas that can spark new desires or modify them, or reveal those which had been buried under the impossibility of satisfying them. This is why feminism often leads to bisexual or homosexual desire. It is not a decision: it is the lifting of a taboo. The radical lesbians acknowledge this implicitly, if they agree with the woman who wrote: 'At that time, I had not yet discovered my homosexuality.' If one can discover it, it means that it is already there to be discovered, and it is not a political decision like joining a political party. What political activist could say 'At that time, I was on the right, I had not yet discovered my socialism'? The 'choice' of lesbianism implies an existent desire, probably unconscious or maybe less strong at that time than an also-present heterosexual desire. The radical lesbians are fully aware of this and talk about the 'repressed homosexuality of heterosexual women' – which presupposes their acceptance of the notion of the unconscious – which in turn has no meaning at all if one claims to be able to 'choose' one's desires.

That many women – maybe all, although at the moment I don't think so (but then I don't know) – have unconscious homosexual desires, I find quite plausible. That these desires are, in most cases, never allowed to come to light because of the dominant heterosexual norm is, I think, equally convincing. However this does not mean that one can *choose* to feel physical desire for women or stop feeling desire for men.

The notion of political choice implies that lesbians could, if they so chose, desire men. To turn desire into a voluntary decision is to remove all meaning from it. To say that all women have, or could have, the same desires is to deny each woman's individuality, her particularity, which comes from an inextricable blend of the dominant culture and her personal history (and it is because this culture evolves, because her history continues and can change direction, that new desires are born). Of course, homosexuality is not a 'different sexuality' – not for the reasons given by separatism, but simply because all sexualities are different. There are as many types of sexuality as there are individuals, and as many different sexual relationships as there are relationships between individuals; there are forms of heterosexuality as there are forms of homosexuality, which is demonstrated, in spite of 'normalizing', 'uniformity-creating' patriarchy, by the diversity of texts on sexuality, homosexual and heterosexual. It is also demonstrated by the fact that radical lesbians do not want to be associated with 'club-going lesbians'. There can be much more in common between one type of homosexual relationship and one kind of heterosexual relationship than between two heterosexual relationships, etc.

If homosexuality is nothing but a bodily practice linked to homo-sociality, if desire is removed from it, than sexuality dies. If desire is not something you *feel*, which takes you sometimes by surprise, then how do you explain that you feel desire for a *particular person* and not for someone else? If you can choose to desire women rather than men, it should follow that you can choose to desire blondes rather than brunettes, tall women rather than small ones, etc. People become interchangeable: you can desire whom you choose, but you choose not to desire oppressors. This is not what the radical lesbians say, but it is the logical result of their position, and it is a dangerous logic: it ends up the same as patriarchal ideology which is based on lack of distinction, on the idea that there is something called 'woman'. This image is supported by left wing men for whom sexual freedom means 'make love with whoever you want'. The feminist assertion, on the other hand, is that we desire individuals for what they are; that they are not interchangeable; and that there are some people we do not desire and cannot desire. Desire goes hand in hand with lack of desire: deny the first and the second disappears. What makes rape, unwanted attention, or the forced marriages that women still suffer in so many countries so appalling is the fact that they are the denial of the lack of desire.

Should we be surprised to read Monique Wittig's separatist arguments, in which she uses the same words about heterosexual women that the worst male chauvinist would use about women: 'one aspect of lesbian oppression is that women are out of our reach because they belong to men'? And so, a 'feminist' starts to talk about women as if they were purely passive, objects over which men and 'non-women' fight, with no initiative or will of their own. As for me, when I hear that we are 'out of reach' because we 'belong to men', it has the same effect as when Senator Henriet said we were of more use in bed than in politics.[3] And if there is a difference between these two attitudes, I am still waiting for someone to point it out, because, quite honestly, I can't find it. It is also a ridiculous position, because it implies that one is heterosexual without really wanting to be, but lesbian by choice. What happens to the very notion of choice when there is no alternative?

Resistance, collaborators, kapos – these are the terms that radical lesbians use to talk about this problem. Because they fail to analyse sexual oppression in its complexity and its specificity, radical lesbians are obliged to replace our concrete reality – which doesn't fit into their schemas – by recourse to the imagination, to fit women into the stories of other peoples' oppressions rather than bringing our own history to light. This is why it is important to criticize this theory: stripped of pertinence, it doesn't bring us anything to use in our struggle for our liberation.

On the other hand, it is essential not only to demand the right to be a lesbian, and to have the right to control our own bodies, but to make it possible for women's homosexual desires to come to light. It is in feminists' interests, whoever they are, to sow disorder, in every possible way, in sex categories which serve as legitimation for the oppressive division of individuals.

Notes and references

1   The original title was 'Ah, je ris de me voir si belle en ce miroir' (Ah, I laugh to see my beautiful reflection in this mirror). Dhavernas objects to the notion that all women are identical reflections of each other. See p. 106.

2   These women, some of whom have been mentioned before, have, on the whole, a positive approach to women's difference and have worked on sexuality and difference as seen through women's relationships to language and to writing. *Sorcières* (witches) was a literary review which focused on this relationship.

3   Senator Henriet spoke against women's right to vote and expressed the common anxiety about France's low birth rate.

7 Party politics: women and the left

Many of the women who became involved in the MLF after the events of May '68 were already involved in mixed left-wing political groups – not, on the whole in mainstream parliamentary political parties but in groups of the 'revolutionary' left. These included the anarchist *mouvement du 22 mars* (22 March Movement), named after a day when a number of its members were arrested; the anarchist *Situationnistes Internationales* (International Situationists);[1] the Maoist *Gauche Prolétarienne* (Proletarian Left); and the Trotskyist *Ligue Communiste Révolutionnaire* (Revolutionary Communist League).

These so-called 'alternative' groups, eclectic in composition and in theory, shared one element that alienated many women members: while they believed in liberating the working class or maybe the Third World, they failed to notice the oppression of women. Male revolutionaries refused to consider that women's oppression existed as such, and needed to be accounted for in the development of any new or existent theory. They also refused to modify their behaviour where women were concerned, and women inside the organization, or linked with male revolutionaries emotionally, continued to find themselves treated in traditional and patronizing ways.

When the MLF seemed to offer a new kind of politics, many disaffected women left mixed political groups altogether in favour of organizing with other women only. Others were less certain that they wanted no part of mixed political organizations, and wanted to retain some kind of affiliation with their former group. They tended to be drawn to the 'class-struggle current' in the MLF. This current included women who wanted some link with mixed groups, whether it was in terms of seeing feminism as part of the class struggle, or exploring the connection between feminism and socialism from a standpoint of feminist autonomy. Within this current, the focus tended to be on whether or not capitalism was the main enemy,[2] the relation of capitalism to patriarchy, the exploitation of women at work, and the burden of the double shift (first in paid – usually badly-paid – employment and then unpaid in the home). While other groups of feminists believed that all women share a common oppression based on gender, 'class-struggle' feminists were less sure that middle-class women were oppressed as well, and did not subscribe to the sex-class theory of radical feminists.

The 'class-struggle current' included too many diverging political positions for it to be able to maintain a coherent existence for very long, and after about 1976–77, feminists in France stopped talking in terms of these different currents: small groups of like-minded women continued to meet, work on various projects and join together from time to time for an event or a demonstration, but sweeping revolutionary projects were increasingly abandoned. This was true not just for feminists, but for the French left as a whole, the further away they moved from May '68.[3]

Women members of the *Parti Communiste Français* (PCF – the French Communist Party) and the *Parti Socialiste* (PS – the French Socialist Party) had a different experience. They obviously did not share the anti-institutional ideas of the MLF, for whom the difference between a 'movement' and an 'institution' was all-important. In her autobiography, Yvette Roudy, Minister for Women's Rights in the Socialist government, wrote that the feminists within trade unions and political parties and women in the MLF despised each other[4] in spite of recognizing that they had certain ideas in common. Women in the MLF felt that once you were caught within the institution of a party or a union, the structural constraints would make any real radical change impossible. Women within political parties felt, as Huguette Bouchardeau (Minister of the Environment in the Socialist government) said, that whatever we feel about political parties, they form the medium by which change can be effected, and if women do not fight within the established political arena, they will be forgotten and ignored.[5]

Even so, feminists inside the PCF and the PS have not found it easy to raise the consciousness of their party brothers. The PCF, in particular, is a highly centralized organization in which disagreement is practically impossible once a political decision has been made. In 1975, the PCF began to call itself the 'party of women's liberation'[6] and loudly proclaimed its good track record as far as numbers of women members, activists, candidates, committee members, etc. were concerned. They did not remind women that they had stood against the legalization of contraception and abortion until very late in the day[7] because they did not want working-class women to adopt the same vices as middle-class women, nor did they mention their homophobia. In 1978, a group of Communist women set up a collective called *Elles Voient Rouge* (Women See Red) and produced a magazine by the same name (see the first extract, pp. 116–19). Their first declaration, 'Le parti communiste mis à nu par ses femmes' (The Communist Party exposed by its women), was offered to the party newspaper *Humanité*, which refused to print it. The women then gave it to *Le Monde* which published it on 12 June 1978. The collective found itself attacked and ridiculed by party faithful. The PCF could not accept criticism from inside its own ranks, and while the feminists were not actually thrown out of the party, their cards were not renewed.

The PS has had a different structure and a different history. Founded in 1969 and merging with some socialist and centre-left political clubs[8] in 1971, it has always consisted of several currents with differing theoretical approaches to socialism. For instance, the CERES current (*Centre d'Etudes de Recherches et d'Éducation Socialistes* – Centre for socialist studies, research and education) which is (or at any rate, was) committed to self-management (*autogestion*), while another current wanted strong links with the PCF; some currents called themselves Marxist, while others repudiated Marxism in favour of social democracy. There were feminists in all currents, women who believed that the PS did not take women seriously either as political beings or in terms of their theory. In other words, they had the same complaint as communist feminists and as feminist 'revolutionaries'. A group of socialist feminists decided to use the PS system to try and bring women on to the socialist political agenda, and formed a current. It was eventually known as the *courant G* because it was seventh on the agenda of proposals for and by different currents at the Socialist Party Congress in 1978. It needed 5 per cent of votes at Congress to be accepted as a current nationally which would be represented within PS leadership: it received less than 1 per cent. None the less, the feminist current was represented at local level, and it too produced a magazine.[9] When the current eventually folded, after the 1981 elections, it was for a variety of reasons internal to the group rather than because of hostility to the group from outside.

The second extract in this section is from the PS feminist magazine and is of particular interest because it was written after the Socialists came to power in 1981. It was made very clear that power-sharing with feminists was not viable; that while in opposition, lip-service could be paid to feminism, but once in power, a feminism that contested party policy was not to be tolerated. The women who occupied the posts in the Ministry for Women's Rights were not from the *courant G* – Yvette Roudy had indeed spoken out against the feminist current as being divisive. The position of women within the PS does not seem to be improving, and the March 1986 elections, which introduced proportional representation into France, found women candidates at the bottom of electoral lists and hardly likely to be elected.[10]

The third piece on this issue is an article written by Elaine Viennot and published in *Nouvelles Questions Féministes* in 1981. The article traces the path trodden by many feminists in their difficult relationship with political parties of any kind. Her own experience was with a 'revolutionary' organization, and she follows through the different stages of this allegiance, and raises the problems, disappointments and contradictions, with a humour and an irony born of experience. Written at a time when strong arguments were being made for closer links between the MLF and the Socialist government, Viennot's article is a reminder of the pitfalls and the compromises that accompany involvement with traditional politics and with power.

Notes and references

1   An anarchist group influenced by surrealism.
2   See Christine Delphy, *Close to Home* (Hutchinson, 1984), pp. 57–77.
3   Some observers maintain that the move from revolutionary idealism to a more pragmatic approach to politics was the change that brought the Socialists to power: former revolutionaries began to accept the political game as it was already being played.
4   Yvette Roudy, *A Cause d'elles* (Albin Michel, 1985), pp. 114–5.
5   In *Tribune Socialiste*, 14 December 1978 newspaper of the PSU (Unified Socialist Party), of which Bouchardeau was national secretary until April 1985.
6   In French, this was *parti de libération de la femme*, that is, the party of *woman's* liberation, not women's liberation. This showed that the PCF had no real idea about feminism, as in the MLF, *la femme* was always specifically rejected in favour of *des femmes*. This indicated a move from considering women as all the same and as unchanging, to, as Delphy pointed out in her article (pp. 33, above), 'beings of flesh and blood'.
7   Contraception was legalized in 1967 and François Mitterrand was the first

political figure to support it in a presidential election (1965). Abortion was made legal in some cases in 1974.

8 The political clubs were a forum for debate and discussion of theory and were not parties as such. They flourished in the 1960s (although they began in the French Revolution and have been a sporadic part of French political life ever since) but have lost importance at the time of writing.

9 Called *Mignonnes, allons voir sous la rose*, a play on a poem by the sixteenth-century poet Ronsard, this title calls for women to examine what lies under the Socialist rose rather than simply looking at it.

10 With proportional representation, each party puts forward a number of names according to how many seats are available in each Département in France. Should the PS win, say, 48 per cent of the vote in any given Département, it would be allotted seven (for instance) seats out of the fifteen available. The first seven names on the PS list would thus be elected, and the remaining eight would not. Women's names tend to be low on the list. There are thirty-three women in the new National Assembly, a drop from 5.9 per cent to 5.5 per cent. The number of Socialist women has, however, increased significantly.

Feminist and communist*

The *Elles Voient Rouge* collective

We have become feminists through our everyday struggles in our social, emotional and sexual lives. We have become feminists also thanks to the women's liberation movement. Feminism has brought out a new contradiction for us in our political practice: we have to define ourselves not only in relation to capitalism, but also in relation to sexism (including the sexism of our comrades in the party). We therefore have to fight a 'war on two fronts', and this war has pushed us towards organizing as women in the context of our political organization, in order to develop our own analyses, to try and define what we want to say, to impose on the party, to shake things up in the party. Is it still really a question of 'demanding' a few reforms, demanding to be taken into account and to be acknowledged – or is it not rather a question of engaging in an out-and-out struggle?

This 'out-and-out struggle' is politically significant and should open our eyes to the role feminism plays in a revolution. It means that sexism isn't just a question of 'attitudes' or of 'mentality' or even simply of the 'site' of oppression, but it is an entire *system* and that fighting a system requires more than just demands, even though they too are necessary. This system is *patriarchy*, which capitalism uses for its own benefits and which itself benefits from capitalism.

This 'out-and-out struggle' concerns us specifically as feminist activists inside a political party. For a start, why are we even involved in a political party? Because we believe that a revolutionary struggle against the State can only take place within a working-class revolutionary organization which takes power. The 'out-and-out struggle' therefore means that we have to engage in a particular struggle within political organizations so

*From *Elles Voient Rouge*, no. 0, 1979.

that feminism can take its rightful place, as part and parcel of the revolutionary struggle.

Finally, 'out-and-out' means that there can be no revolution without the transformation of relations between men and women, between women, throughout society and especially in the working class. A revolution which represses women's struggle in any way can only be – and will inevitably be – incomplete.

Feminism is the force that allows us to engage in this out-and-out revolutionary combat, in which we, as communists, believe.

Patriarchy and capitalism

What then, in more precise terms, does it mean to be a feminist? Is it simply an 'attitude'? We think not: we think feminism is an ideological and political choice. It has a precise theoretical basis, which incorporates:

1 Patriarchy, being the power that men exercise over women. This power is both ideological and economic. It determines the specific oppression that operates in general 'sexist' masculine and feminine practices whose goal is to perpetuate against all odds the appropriation of women by men – until more subtle methods are found. Furthermore, it depends on economic exploitation, based on women's unpaid domestic labour, on the gendered division of waged labour in capitalism (unequal salaries, unequal opportunities, etc.).

A revolutionary feminist recognizes the simultaneous oppression and exploitation exercised in conjunction by patriarchy and capitalism. She tries to analyse how they operate together and reproduce each other, just as all State systems reproduce, and are reproduced by, patriarchy. Only recognition of the complicity between the two systems will allow us to develop a Marxist and therefore revolutionary analysis of exploitation and its power system. Attempting to bypass this theoretical basis, that is, this feminist perspective, is to engage in an incomplete, inconsequential, opportunist political, ideological and economic struggle.

2 When we talk about *domestic labour*, we are talking about the family as the main site of the production and reproduction of patriarchy. The family is not the 'refuge', the 'haven', as people on both the left and the right enjoy telling us. It doesn't escape the 'state of war' that exists everywhere in society, a state of war that is constantly masked and hidden by this ideology of 'family love' and 'security' (safety from outside attacks) which

traps women and keeps them subordinate. Just lift the veil of the family a little and what do you find? What role is assigned to women? How are little girls and little boys brought up? What is domestic labour all about, seeing that even waged women take on what is called the 'double daily shift'?

It is easy to see that family emotional ties are far from 'natural', but are created by patriarchal ideology and are one of its cornerstones. The family's role in the reproduction of capital explains the rigour with which the capitalist system tries to send women back to the home.

Sending women back to the home has two advantages: first, an economic advantage: it reduces unemployment figures, and it reduces the cost of reproducing the workforce by making women work unpaid to keep their husband and their children. Second, it has an ideological and political advantage: it perpetuates divisions between working-class men and women and stops women from organizing together to fight their exploitation by patriarchy and capitalism. It makes working women guilty by making them responsible for the State's failures. For instance children's failure at school is blamed not on lack of adequate funding but on mothers not being at home for their children. The family is used as a shock absorber for social conflicts.

Most importantly, and here we see the practical strength of patriarchal ideology, is that this power politics finds *objective accomplices* in men. Men think it's 'normal' for women to stay at home, 'normal' that they bring up the kids, 'normal' that they do unpaid housework, 'normal' that women's waged work is less important than their own. And many women, brought up believing in this 'normality', reproduce it.

We also have to recognize the fact that the development of capital and the all-important role of the State in controlling the economic and ideological processes of capitalism, reshapes the face of patriarchy by integrating it into a wider system and into new institutions – for instance into schooling. School, like the family, guarantees the basis of children's education and thereby allows patriarchal ideology to be reproduced.

3 Finally, a revolutionary feminist is a materialist, that is, rejects the idea of 'feminine nature', of any natural 'destiny' or 'role' particularly when it takes the shape of the biological justification of oppression.

Feminist and communist, we therefore have to fight on two fronts. Fight the patriarchal system and name our objective oppressors: men. This system, which manipulates men and women, divides us and weakens our revolutionary strength. We have to fight capitalism, and these two fronts cannot be separated. Most fundamentally, we women have to fight the sexist ideology and practices in all power systems, in all the new and old forms of the class struggle. Patriarchy existed long before capital, has survived and adapted to different modes of production, has continued through all revolutions, exists in 'socialism' where it obstinately perpetuates the same hierarchy between men and women and therefore the same power structures.

In order to be proper feminists and proper communists, in other words, revolutionary, we have to forget this 'two fronts' business which makes us communists here (and not feminists) and feminists there (and not communists) – another division of labour dividing us. This doesn't mean that we don't believe in an autonomous women's liberation movement outside political organizations; of course we do, it is essential and it is essential that we are part of it. But for us the issue is that we must be feminist *and* communist wherever we are.

We aren't, as Georges Marchais and Madeleine Vincent[1] claim, happy in the party. A political party isn't miraculously protected from the dominant ideology. How could we be 'happy' when other people speak on our behalf instead of us?

To say that there is no problem in the party where women are concerned is to silence us, to bury us in the name of a theoretical 'equality' without even examining what is really happening. This notion of equality operates in the party as it does in bourgeois ideology (from which it comes), it hides our real oppression and shuts our mouths before we have time to open them.

This is why we are speaking out. This is why, in the face of so many speeches and so much silence (speeches hide silence) we believe it is necessary to clarify our positions, and call on other women, more and more women, to join us in our questioning.

Notes and references

1 George Marchais is the Party Secretary, and Madeleine Vincent is the PCF's 'political bureau' spokeswoman on women's affairs and 'women's condition'. The PCF has claimed since 1975 to be the party for women's liberation.

Patriarchy in the *Parti Socialiste* (Socialist Party)*

In the 1981 National Assembly:[1] sixteen women among 269 Socialist Deputies (MPs). The advance of the PS benefited ten times more men than women: 148 new male MPs – fourteen new women.

The PS, which denounces inequality and oppression, is not up to respecting equality between men and women in its own ranks.

The party practises the exclusion of women. It is a men-only party because men have all the power in it. In theory there is equality of opportunity and of rights in the party at all levels but, like everywhere else, the higher you get in the hierarchy, the closer you get to power, the fewer women you see. These structures do not allow for real democratic functioning. How can the Socialist Party go on claiming the theoretical equality of rights while in reality it maintains oppression!

Men's power in the party is based on: discourse, where women's words are denied as soon as they depart from traditional discourse; behaviour of men who use women for the single goal of power in the rivalry between the currents; the organization of the party itself: first, with its typically patriarchal structures based on hierarchy and centralization; second, with its selective, sexist 'democracy'.

We are told that it is the democratic functioning of the party that is stopping women from becoming more powerful. We, on the other hand, say that if a mode of functioning reproduces oppression, it is because, contrary to its appearance, it is not democratic. It is, therefore, the functioning and not the results that must be questioned. We disagree with the idea that democracy means the law of the greatest number alone. Having a majority has never, of itself, guaranteed democratic political positions (for

* Extract from the political proposal of the *courant G*, the women's current in the PS (1981).

example, Fascism, Nazism). There is no example of oppressed groups, even in large numbers, who have been able to overcome the oppressive nature of a party structure. This structure in fact reinforces exclusion, silence, marginalization, and therefore oppression. It reduces to the status of minority those who have not had the chance to escape from the weight of the structures that are crushing them.

We should point out that the 'democratic' and patriarchal structures of the Socialist Party are directing it towards an authoritarian socialism and the reinstating of absolute power that doesn't allow new political ideas and strengths to come out. A substantial rethinking of the idea of democracy, its contents and the way it operates, is urgent.

As for analysis of patriarchal oppression, well the Socialist Party hasn't undertaken one any more than it has decided to fight patriarchy in society as a whole or inside the party. And how could it be otherwise in a party composed mostly by men. As men, they don't want to acknowledge that they are oppressors: as socialists, they can't admit this without being in contradiction with their ideology. It is easier for them to hide women's oppression and to shut up those women who are trying to make them face their contradictions.

A few vague declarations of intent, a few proposals tacked on to the end of chapters, have never replaced political analysis. This is the basic vice of the socialist project.

And yet the struggle against patriarchy implies a 'radical break' – and there can be no socialism without that radical break.

Autonomy

It is up to women to formulate women's politics. We want to take our perspective as oppressed people as our starting point, and not our oppressors' perspective.

1 A common political identity: our political identity is defined by the oppression and exploitation of all women. Our structural and political autonomy is based on this common identity, that is prior to all others and cannot be reduced to all others, as our oppression is not the same thing as the class struggle.
2 Rejection of a selective, sexist 'democracy': in 1791, the Constituent Assembly[2] reserved the right to vote for those with money (selective suffrage). This suffrage was the basis for a 'democracy' which nevertheless

excluded the majority of male citizens and all female citizens.

The mode of operation of our national institutions, called democratic, in reality excludes almost all women citizens from access to power, discriminating against them on the basis of their sex. For example: 90 per cent of the government is formed by men; 95 per cent of the National Assembly are men. We find similar percentages at the top of our political parties and our trade unions.

Women never control what happens to their struggles. They never make the decisions that concern them. When the demands expressed by women during their struggles (abortion, equality, etc.) are turned into laws, they are in fact selected, taken up only partially or deformed (such as the abortion law) or rejected by decision-making bodies made up mostly of men.

We now have to find a way for women to control things, just as we found a way to talk about worker control. We must find a way that allows women to make the decisions that concern their lives, just as we found a way to talk about self-management.

One of the first steps in this direction is a quota of a 50 per cent maximum of men in all the elected assemblies in France (Parliament, regional, departmental and local assemblies) which would mean that they couldn't take hold of all the power and would allow for an equal distribution of power.

Inside the party

We demand a maximum of 50 per cent men in all the decision-making levels of the party. Yet even this isn't enough; women must have an autonomous organization within the party in which they get together at all levels of the party to formulate policies concerning women. They will study all the party's texts and proposals, will put forward counter-proposals and will then negotiate them in the different committees composed of equal numbers of men and women. They alone will appoint their representatives at the different levels in the party and will select candidates for election at both national and local level. Only then will women be recognized as fully-fledged political partners.

The current party organization, with its 'National Secretary for Women's Struggles' and its 20 per cent quota, is a cop out. We don't want the support of one woman appointed by the men of whichever mainstream current it may be; we want women to approve every measure, every step taken.

Autonomy goes hand in hand with a political project, otherwise it would just be another separatism, based on sex. This is why our practice today is expressed in this proposal, and our political priority: the destruction of patriarchy.

Our alternative politics is radical, global. In its analysis and in its practice, it is the only one able to remove the weight of patriarchy that hangs over socialism, and to open in every sphere the way towards changes that we can't even imagine today.

Notes and references

1 The National Assembly is the French House of Commons. Members of Parliament are called Deputies.
2 The Constituent Assembly in 1791 was set up in order to draft a Constitution for the First French Republic during the Great Revolution.

Feminism and political parties: the impossible union*

Eliane Viennot

Over the last ten years many women have felt that it might be possible to operate a feminist transformation inside their political organization. Up to now, wherever this attempt has been made, the result has been failure, always ending with feminists being 'pushed out'. It seems to me that this failure is largely due to insuperable structural obstacles concerning mixed groups. Later I'll come back to this point. But first I'd like to shed some light on the way that women involved in political organizations become radicalized, in order to show that part of the mistrust felt towards them by women in the Women's Liberation Movement (MLF) is largely based on simply not understanding their experience, or on oversimplifying it.[1] MLF women tend to assimilate these women to their party . . . that is, we ultimately refuse to consider them as women like us, who have their own contradictions.

I would like to show that the radicalizing process involves a certain dynamic of conflict with political institutions – a dynamic which follows certain patterns in all cases and is therefore valid when discussing this 'general' theme. To do this, I will use my own experience in a political group,[1] which, like many others, can be described as having, first, an official line on women's oppression and on the need for their emancipation, and second, direct involvement inside the women's movement. As a group which had ideological and physical proximity to the MLF (it was one of the more 'libertarian' of the far-left groups), it experienced a particularly rapid and intense development of the contradictions associated with feminism. Even so, although different political parties and organizations gain a feminist consciousness according to their

* From *Nouvelles Questions Féministes*, no. 2, October 1981.

own, specific features, I think that once this process is under way, it undergoes the same phases in its development, induces the same modification of the political principles which decide the level of women's participation in high-ranking posts, and finally leads women to the same impossible situation – and it doesn't matter what left-wing party they are in.[2]

Phase one: the era of 'capable women', or the dream of high office

This is the golden age of egalitarianism. In their struggle against the old world and against reactionaries, progressives assert: 'Women are equal to men. They are socially and culturally disadvantaged, of course, but to use this to justify their absence from important political positions would be simply reactionary.' These words ring pleasantly in women's ears: they are not identified with their social handicap'; they are like everyone else. They still don't realize that 'like everyone else' means 'like men': what they want is the human, the universal. Women are equal to men.

This principle might seem a little stale these days. Only the least disadvantaged got anywhere: single, intellectual, impeccable May '68 credentials; most of the time, the fact that they are women is forgotten: they have the same strident tones, the same self-confidence, the same ease in using abstract concepts as men. Some of them are beautiful, brilliant – they might even have the edge over the (not always so clever) men they are dealing with. Yes indeed, these women are equal to men. And the others? The others don't count. 'Women', as has always been the case, are an anonymous, massive, shapeless, transparent group. Only these few women are visible – which is proof enough of *their* equality. Exceptional women, women who have got ahead – women who are also indispensable, foglights in the dark, proving to others that the 'natural lack of ability' that keeps them down is not inevitable for women. *Those* women can do it, therefore women can do it, and so can I? I can become visible, be a leader (another way of becoming visible is to be a leader's wife) whenever I want, I just have to want to enough. Those with confidence try it. They reject the inevitability of roles assigned to women and throw themselves into the fray, trying to change things at once, now: this is the route that feminism takes. The others do the opposite, entrench themselves in principled non-participation: this is also a route that feminism takes. But because they have not understood that women's oppression *does* exist and takes many forms, or because they haven't understood that women political activists are still women, the different women judge each other unsparingly, calling those who refuse responsibility cowards and those who take it on, sell-outs.

And men still rule OK, satisfied with their principle that gives them a clear conscience without making them share their power. 'Equal responsibility for equal ability' they never get tired of saying, without really worrying that only 5 to 10 per cent of women have 'equal ability'. This was the general position of left-wing political parties and all far-left organizations before the MLF began to make itself felt.

Phase two: from the dream to reality

In fact, if the MLF hadn't been pushing from behind, there is no doubt that this situation could have lasted for years, centuries. But the MLF *does* exist, it questions, provokes, gives us energy. Women who are not content with recognition from the men inside the party, go and look in the MLF for something more and come back completely shaken up. For a while, women participate in both MLF and political organization, each insulated from the other, parallel. But ideas and doubts both take root: women begin to wonder about the purpose of women leaders – don't they merely serve to hide the oppression of other women? And women realize that it isn't enough to decree that men and women are equal for reality to change. Women's oppression has to be taken into account, and for that, it has to be formulated, put into words, by those whom it concerns – themselves! But then something curious – and yet banal – happens. Quite quickly, those who had gone to find their confidence and their courage in the MLF find themselves rewarded and promoted to positions of responsibility in their mixed organization. It isn't quite a strategy to shut them up, although some cynical male leaders find the situation amusing – no, it's more simple than that. The organization needs people with determination, to train other activists, those who have enough consciousness of 'long term interests' to accept administering the daily shit. Rebels are always good at that.

The MLF then becomes an important 'front for intervention' for the organization, which is incapable of letting a social movement develop without sending in its troops in order to 'take it over'. Women's status in the organization suddenly rises: women must be given the tools for their work, trained and accustomed to leadership. At this point, a misunderstanding arises. What the organization wants is for its women activists to infiltrate the MLF, spread the correct political line, keep out other organizations – in short, to recruit, and, whether this was explicitly said or not, to form a 'women's section' linked to the organization in the great Leninist tradition. The Women's Movement (the word 'Liberation' has disappeared) was a historic opportunity, a gift given by the political situation, permitting the organization to strengthen its 'foothold' in society, to widen its base. The women activists try hard. It doesn't work very well, but they do bring from the MLF new recruits (feminists), the habit of collective work, and new ideas. Emboldened by their newly-acquired importance, they write, they talk: about their comrades' sexism, about rampant sexism, about scandalous discrimination. They talk about 'women's oppression' but never mention their own. It is a long time before women leaders talk about their own oppression, they don't dare, don't dare even *think* about it. For the moment, they *represent* the other women in the organization, they are the spokeswomen of the revolt. Unlike the women of the previous 'generation' they have been promoted *because of* their feminism, and their presence in responsible office keeps that particular torch burning. This is the phase when, pushed on by feminists, the organization makes some women specialize in this one task: watching out for signs of contradictions between men and women, centralizing 'work on women', making all activists aware of this work and take it on board. This is the era when the organization adopts the principle that 'Where there is equal ability, priority goes to women.'

It is the era of good intentions.

Phase three: from oppression to struggle

Feminists are nibbling away at the terrain. Rank and file women here, well-known women there; women leaders who had not spoken up until now join them. But the organization can absorb all this. After the speakers have finished speaking at any meeting, the token feminist will politely be asked to give the 'feminist point of view' on the question being discussed. No one figures this out, least of all women. They oblige, uneasily, glad to be useful but also irritated: why does the speaker not bother to think about this point of view himself in his little speech? Yet when some of them try, they don't quite get the point; or else they're paternalistic; or they distort the meaning of what feminists say; impossible. Unbearable. Whole sections of the organization go on ignoring feminism, joking about what they (men and women) blithely call a cultural-movement-of-Parisian-middle-class-intellectuals, without stopping to think about the way they are repeating right-wing abuse, word for word. It is at National Conferences that women become aware of how isolated, marginalized, barely tolerated they are. Feminists are ghosts, work on women flounders.

However, there is no shortage of texts, directives, circulars, anger. But the organization resists, like a large solid immobile lump. Feminists are not up against 'lack of understanding' – it is a question of conflicting political and social interests. Feminism disturbs ways of thinking, questions the content of political 'lines', questions attitudes which had previously been thought of as neutral. For feminists, the time for talking and explaining is over, it is time for gathering troops: it is a time for counter-attack, not for complaints. Using their recently-acquired authority, learned in the organization, women call for women-only meetings, forming groups not for discussion but to act directly as pressure groups.

Of course, some women are not keen; many are half-hearted. But most feminists in the organization, those who form the bulk of the organization's 'intervention' in the MLF, and who were despairing of anything ever coming out of the polite discussions about feminism between leaders, throw themselves into the fight. They suddenly feel invincible. This is the era of the putsch, of bombs thrown in the middle of meetings, of virulent angry tracts: 'Where there is equal ability, priority goes to women.' What does 'equal ability' mean anyway? Male criteria! Women do things differently, talk and plan in a different way, engage in politics differently: the socialism women dream of is warmer, more inventive; women are the real revolutionaries.

This is the era of intense mobilization, when groups of all kinds are formed, speech is liberated, the unsayable is said. The oppression felt by all women activists is now identified, exposed, it overflows. From single mothers, stuck with their problems of childcare to single women without children who are not treated as real women, from working-class women who just want to escape from their lives to the intellectuals called upon by the organization to 'enter' factories, from leaders' wives, denied as individuals, to women leaders, denied as women, from those kept in the role of 'feminist avant-garde' to those who are considered incapable of revolt (women immigrants, older women, schoolgirls), there emerges a many-sided vision of women's oppression, which shows that what divides women is not as important as what unites them, and it shows it explosively. This is the time of the greatest illusion of all: they are determined to do the impossible – make a political organization feminist. It will either be a success, or the end.

Phase four: back to oppression

A power vacuum always provokes the most intense debates. But these vacuums never last very long and men have their own accounts to settle, positions to fight over, power to reconquer. At this point, feminists begin to understand that there is no point in fighting for two or three more women in positions of power, but that we must demand numerical equality with men at every level in the hierarchy. 50 per cent more women means 50 per cent fewer men, if I'm not mistaken. Women's Leninist convictions have been shaken, their lives have been shaken by their experience in the women's movement, and they are now casting a critical glance at the need for an avant-garde at all. The leaders are furious. Between the troubled waters of the private and the low blows of the political, they are trying to regain lost ground. And institutions, even revolutionary ones, never get tired of bringing out the same old chestnuts when they need them. To your left, the labour movement: feminists are intellectuals, all they ever do is criticize, criticize everything without getting involved. They want to destroy the organization. They are the mainstay of the bourgeoisie – and besides, they are all middle class themselves (howls, here, in the name of the working class, from middle-ranking party cadres). To your right, division: feminists want to speak on behalf of all women; they want to get elected on the backs of women; all they want is power.

These blows hurt. Many women, who hadn't been happy about the fuss made by feminists, see this as the right time to express their disagreement: they don't want to be thought of primarily as 'women'. They want to be thought of as individuals, recognized as such, judged on their ability, elected because right for the job and not because they are women (go back to square one, do not pass Go). They are alienated by the feminist monopoly over everything concerning 'women's issues', by the models of liberation that feminists unwittingly provide and that men support. They don't identify with these women who claim to speak for all women. All the organization needs now, for its tactical ends, is to find two or three working-class women to launch an offensive, two or three guilt-ridden intellectuals to support their attack, and it's in the bag.

The phase of polite indifference is over. Now it's war: feminists must be crushed, they are a public danger, scapegoats to blame for everything that's wrong. The joyful feminist advance is abruptly cut short. But – crushing feminists means the end of the democratic conception of political struggle; there are no more chinks in the armour of dogmatism, no hope of seeing imagination win out over organization. It is an ideological, political out-and-out struggle which sets up opposing camps, and men and women line up on both sides. The trap closes. Men on both sides – allies and enemies of feminism – engage in a general political debate, using feminism as an example: women's real oppression is swept under the carpet, forgotten by some, blocked out by others, because every display of weakness on one side is fuel to the argument of the other.

Did we fight so hard to end up with this? From my own experience, I would like to draw out some lessons which may have some general bearing on the conditions of feminist struggles inside political parties and organizations.

First, there are the conditions in which feminist demands are made and how they evolve, which vary according to different types of party. You have to distinguish between those parties and organizations which, in various ways, claim to be feminist, and those which don't breathe a word about it. It seems as though the best way for a political group to avoid problems with its women members is to avoid having an official line on women. This indicates not that women are not oppressed inside these groups (which isn't even worth discussing) but that, for feminist demands to be made in the first place, a certain *space*, a political recognition that the problem exists and is important, is required – as well as some kind of margin of manoeuvre for women in the group.

It is the shape that this space takes that creates a further distinction between groups: on the one hand, there are those parties which, while recognizing that women are subject to a specific oppression, and accepting the need to do something about it, don't know about (or ignore) the MLF, or treat it like an enemy. These parties (the Socialist Party and the Unified Socialist Party in the first case, the Communist Party in the second) have seen the growth of feminist demands inside the party; usually isolated, individual criticisms for airing inside the party only; however, when these demands develop and link up with the women's movement, something changes,[3] in the sense that the parties that these women belong to have no policy towards the MLF, and the MLF has no strategy concerning women from political parties. The women involved in this double-fronted activism have a 'different' presence, as 'other' in each place, a kind of exotic identity which applies to them alone – until they organize, in either group, in order actually to *do* something. It seems that in spite of the apparently trouble-free non-interventionist feminist presence on both fronts, it always ends up with one side winning out. Most feminists in the

Communist Party and the Socialist Party have left their party, like the Women See Red collective in the Communist Party, two-thirds of whom did not renew their party membership after running their magazine for two years.

This isn't the case for women whose organization claims to have a strategy concerning the MLF, because they become the direct agents of this strategy. This particular space is terribly complex. Feminists are invested with a mission to accomplish in the women's movement; rejected, in the MLF, as bearers of an outsider's desire to take over; and, at the same time, held in suspicion by their fellow party members as being a destabilizing influence. The constant movement from one group to the other, the intense problems of allegiance that this involves, means that feminists must always affirm and reaffirm their priorities (Who is most important? Are we feminists in a political organization, or are we political activists representing our organization in the MLF?) according to how far the organization reasserts both its right to intervene in mass movements and also its political superiority to these movements.

This situation, with its impossible contradictions, seems paradoxically more solid and lasting than the previous one. Participation in the MLF is, for these women, both their personal choice and the organization's wish: any contradiction they experience can quickly be called 'objective' and blamed on the difficulties caused by the overall political climate. The contradictory nature of belonging both to a movement that insists on its political independence and to an organization which wants to take it over is practically institutionalized, even theorized into a concept of 'dual loyalties' (double bind?) by some women. It is clear that these contradictions can only get worse, and then the only solution is to stop being a feminist. Which is why the great majority of feminists in far-left revolutionary organizations, in their insistence on remaining feminists, and no matter what shape their particular battle took, have only ever found one direction, one way to go: Out.

The last ten years have shown us that, while we have an independent and aggressive feminist movement, there is no way that women who become more sensitized and radicalized as feminists can be involved in mixed political groups. Whether it's because they are tired of being in parties that pay no attention to their feminism (it's too marginal) or because they have had enough of constantly being called to account by their organization, feminists always end up by leaving – it's just a matter of time.

Second, there is the question of division between feminist and non-feminist women inside a mixed group. This question may seem to be pointless and to come from complicated definitions: how do you define a feminist? But the question isn't raised in this way at all. In our society, all the various degrees of feminist consciousness and absence of feminist consciousness co-exist freely. Feminists get together out of political affinity, act together, and each woman who is not part of a group is alone (or free, which I prefer) to respond as she chooses to feminism: free to listen, to come and see, to turn away from it, to wait, to wait for things to 'mature'. As long as feminism is marginal in political parties, espoused by a certain number of women and evolving more or less underground, other women have the time and space to carry on individually, make up their own minds – and for those who don't feel concerned or affected by feminism, there is still no problem.

However, when feminists organize as a *group*, other women are called upon to define themselves in relation to it. Men play a crucial role at this point. As they are forced to choose sides, women choose their position according to their own past, their emotional ties, their loves, their political preferences, either *with* the feminists, or on the *outside*: but it is an outside that isn't an alternative group. On the other hand, once the organization decides not to tolerate feminists inside its ranks and not to take their critique into account (that is, as soon as the organization realizes that its survival is at stake) then it formulates an opposition argument, *against* feminists (and usually very anti-feminist, of course). At this point, all women who aren't part of the feminist group are, whether they like it or not, identified as non-feminists which is intolerable and isn't always related to the substance of the for/against positions held. More than anything else, it is a question of rewards, as it is in any closed, hierarchical system. Symbolic rewards, given out according to how far you are in or out of the group – actual rewards, that is, jobs to fill and to give out (for if feminists are dislodged, there will be jobs to fill). Once certain limits have been reached, feminism can't advance inside a mixed group – or worse, it turns against women by making some of them agents of repression, used to keep it out.

Finally, there is the question of alliances. Women's oppression isn't a detail in the social landscape but one of its most basic features. Feminist demands therefore go beyond the questions of functioning, behaviour, etc. that they usually start from. Or rather, they usually end up by bringing out the fundamental political problems contained within these questions.

This is how almost all feminist groups end up questioning hierarchy, manipulation, avant-gardism, differing ideas about how to sieze power, etc. These issues, which are discussed by feminists, but which aren't specifically feminist issues, inevitably find on the one hand a positive echo from some men who agree with the general problems raised but who aren't exactly feminist; and on the other, a negative echo from some women who disagree over the content of the issues, to the point that all feminist revolt eventually finds itself obliged to form alliances with men against other women. Feminism is thus transformed into a *discourse on* women, losing its real content, which is above all, and beyond everything else, *a practice of solidarity with all women*, whatever their political opinion. Ultimately, women in mixed political groups have to face the following dilemma:

- either they have to limits their demands to the 'defence of specific (women's) interests', so that they can go on addressing all women, and therefore become a kind of trade union – that is, *give up feminism*;
- or they can accept the political consequences of their questions and demands, and thereby run the risk of cutting themselves off from some women, or even find themselves pitted against each other – that is, *stop acting as feminists*.

Whichever way you look at it, you can't get round it.

The contradictions I have just discussed lead me to the following, probably provisional, conclusions:

1 At the moment, women will go on fighting a feminist battle inside political groups; they will also continue participating in the MLF in increasing numbers, as they have done since 1970.
2 Participation in a mixed group can only ever be destructive and contradictory for feminists (which doesn't always mean that it is impossible or wrong). It is most destructive in the more structured groups, whose goals are all-encompassing and on a global scale; but whatever the context and however restrained the activism, participation in a mixed group is destructive and contradictory for still another reason. This is that the socially dominant position held by men, as well as their numerical supremacy in most groups, make them the most important, and means that ideas always circulate via men. When women become aware of this, they create women-only 'free spaces', which are in fact enclaves within the dominant territory, allowing them to react to male excesses, politically incorrect behaviour,

etc. – but which in fact limits them to reacting to what others do. Pressures, deadlines, permanent confrontations with men preclude the possibility of real work being done.

For all these reasons, I believe that even if we still need to learn how to act politically at every level in the movement, even if we don't know how to intervene in every sphere, nor how to think things through, this is what we should be aiming for in our work. Having a women-only movement isn't a guarantee from certain failures that traditional politics have also had. Inside a 'women-only milieu' there are in-groups, groups which want to take over, politically ambitious women, 'party' practices, which are unfortunately as much the prerogative of politically-organized women (past or present) as of others. It seems to me, however, that for the question of divisions among women to be raised in accurate and appropriate terms, a women-only movement seems simply the essential condition – but it has taken me years to get to this 'simply'.

Notes and references

1 Elaine Viennot was a member of *Révolution!*
2 This obviously doesn't apply to parties which don't see the need for sexual equality.
3 For instance *Elles Voient Rouge* in the PCF, and the *courant G* in the PS.

8 Reflections on the women's liberation movement

Françoise Collin's article *Au Revoir* appeared in 1978 in the last issue of the Belgian journal *les cahiers du Grif* before its four year break. Collin ranges widely over issues and questions that have already been raised by other women in this anthology, reinforcing some points of view, bringing new light to others. I think that she asks questions that are fundamental and troubling to all feminists, while keeping in mind the enormous amount that feminism has achieved in a very short space of time.

For instance, in her thinking on difference, Collin rejects the positions that turn the question into a caricature of woman-as-body, as in Annie Leclerc, or the denial of woman's body, as in Guillaumin. Collin explores the contradictions and ambiguities contained within the notion of difference, without simplifying the issue.

Collin also looks at the nature of feminism itself, distinguishing it from 'ideology' or other '-isms', which many women feel is a way of closing up feminism into a reassuring body of thought rather than allowing for its contradictions, diversity and dynamism. She discusses the achievements of the women's movement which, although not always easy to measure, certainly go further than legislative change. She makes a useful distinction between co-option and reform, discussed also by Picq, and she reflects on the defusion and dilution of radicalism that accompanies the diffusion of feminism. Collin asks the question 'How we can be radical today, now that women talking (speaking out, talking together without men) is no longer shocking or considered to be a radical act?'

Françoise Collin therefore returns to themes which are raised again and again in this collection concerning the nature of feminism, the shape of the movement and the way forward. It seems to me that Collin's thinking on her own movement and her own experience is a valuable contribution to a debate on feminism in the 1980s which involves feminists not only in the French-speaking world, but everywhere.

Au Revoir*

Françoise Collin

Feminism: our own critique

We insist on using the word 'feminism' here, out of convenience and out of loyalty, knowing full well that while it has lost its impact through co-option, it has also been rejected by many women in the movement, who don't want to succumb to any of the '-isms' that punctuate the history of male ideologies (Marxism, Christianity, socialism, idealism, materialism, etc.). This position is held by 'intellectuals' in the French-speaking world in particular, who are conscious of the danger inherent in language and careful not to snare their experience and actions in a linguistic trap. The others – 'non-intellectuals' maybe – continue (like us) to use feminism as a kind of catch-all concept that designates, in general terms, the individual and collective work undertaken in order radically to transform women's lives.

If some women regard the concept of feminism with suspicion, it is basically because of its closeness to ideology. The women's movement is not an ideology which, suitably formulated and defined, would set out a new norm for individual and social action, based on an old or new conception of Woman, and leading to a feminist society. This need for theoretical and practical orthodoxy, which masculine thought deplores our lack of and is constantly trying to make us establish, is in fact characteristic of masculine thought itself. To give in to it would, therefore, be to give in to its Order. The women's movement is, above all, resistance to the One and has no wish to replace it with another One. Rejecting this masculine Oneness in favour of many-sided desires and voices, are women in their diversity and their unpredictable differences. This reaction against the (phallocratic) One operates as much in the sphere of professional or private

*From *les cahiers du Grif*, no. 22/23, 1978. This is an edited extract.

life as in what is called cultural practice – writing, speaking, film, painting, sculpture, etc.

From this perspective, political activism itself becomes suspect in that it tends to do away with differences within a militant group, and differences concerning the goal pursued. Activism, implicitly or explicitly, may set up new norms. There is also a certain military element in activism that women dislike – a truly phallic kind of regimentation, discipline and imperialism.

But the conditions of women's lives will not improve and women will not get any closer to their autonomy without taking action, positively and collectively, with the aim of overthrowing the prison-like conditions in which they live at the moment. This action obviously seeks to allow women, in the places and the circumstances that concern them, to make their own choices, and to bring about conditions favourable to this end. The concern is always to open cracks and allow in something different, to break down the monolith.

Woman, women, some women

'What is Woman' then, becomes the wrong question. Over the last few years, we have witnessed the development of consciously or unconsciously 'essentialist' or 'naturalist' arguments and practices, which aim to define woman in relation to man or in relation to the definition that man has given woman (and in a way we can't escape this, as soon as we pronounce the word 'woman'). We see everywhere this oscillation between the assertion of the existence of a female specificity, biological specificity (rooted in a 'biologism' which speaks of blood, of wombs, of body and of writing the body), and the affirmation of the existence of a general bisexuality (rooted in a 'historicism' which sees 'becoming woman' as a decline). We have seen the pitfalls of both arguments: the former, closing women up in a neo-femininity, the latter tending to assimilate women with men.

We know that our thinking is shot through with ambiguity, with contradictions: at one and the same time, we meet as women and define our politics as women (and therefore woman) and we attack this concept as created by dualist, masculine thought. This dualist thought is always suspect because it is always based on hierarchy, on domination (white/black, western/eastern, men/women, etc.) How can we confront this dualism when our starting point is at one of its negative poles? By introducing the 'feminine' into a world that has been purely male up till now?

By the coming of a female world, or a world of women? Will women end up playing the same role in feminist thought that the proletariat plays in Marxist thought; untainted by the system's faults, will they save the human race, create heaven on earth?

We know that they won't. We aren't really trying to save the human race. We want our voices to be heard, our actions to be unconstrained, and our desires not repressed before they can be expressed. Is this pragmatic? Maybe; but with its subversive content intact. We say 'we' so that one day every women can say 'I'. We speak in generalizations (women) to change the way that women are spoken of. We challenge subjectivity in order to reach our individuality. We fight a 'condition' so that we can have an existence.

Our achievements

If we counted only legislative reforms as achievements, then recent direct or indirect feminist achievements, while not negligible, look a bit slim: relative liberalization of abortion in certain countries, the right to divorce in Italy at last, EEC recommendations about employment rights, sale of contraceptives tolerated, etc.

We feel that the women's movement has, none the less, had other effects recently, which, although less easy to pinpoint than a law, we experience constantly. Because of the women's movement women are less isolated, meet each other more easily and identify more with each other when they meet. Women share a sense of complicity in increasing numbers and in wider and wider spheres: obviously they don't always agree with one another, but they talk to each other and are beginning to enjoy living partially or totally with other women. They no longer need the mediation of a man in order to have their own lives. Of course many women resist this movement and continue 'siding' with men, seeking their approval more than anything else. Many are afraid to give themselves to the movement because they are afraid that, in loving women, they will lose men, or men's praise, which they need for various sexual or economic reasons. But even these women 'dip' more and more frequently into the world of women. They all begin by needing women, that is, by needing themselves. Each woman finds that friendship with women is more immediate, more spontaneous, warmer, more lighthearted, more straightforward, more dynamic and more inventive than it is with men, weighed down by their image and their social codes. Going from men to women is like going from a foreign language to a mother tongue (without forgetting that a mother tongue does not exclude misunderstandings and disagreements). This is so much so, that when they go back to the world of men, women sometimes have great trouble finding the words and gestures of this former code.

This ease of communication between women together, this short cut, has encouraged a dynamism among women which is visible in their professional and private lives, and which is expressed in socio-political structures such as political parties and unions. In these, we often witness a double movement: on the one hand, the powers that be create a purely showpiece type of feminism, with opportunistic and electoral goals, and we see the appointment of several more or less aware women to political posts; on the other hand, we see women demanding the right to speak and act autonomously within these structures. These two movements can sometimes accidentally come together and reinforce each other. Their impact, although it is insufficient, is not negligible.

However, action at any level at all is impossible without a personal and collective awareness, in fairly widespread groups, of the problem of being a woman. It is here, at the roots, that the women's movement – feminism – has recently been effective and where it remains absolutely essential. Many (but not all) women are now daring to examine and identify the difficulties in their lives and seek solutions to their problems. They no longer believe that their lives are prescribed. They are growing aware of, and beginning to demand, their rights and make others aware of them; they are beginning to grow aware of, and make visible, their own desires. They are no longer prepared to pay any price to keep their 'security' that is at any rate very precarious.

Young women, brought up by mothers whose consciousness had already been raised, found that some of the groundwork had been done for them. They are already questioning their relation to work, to emotions, asking things that their mothers didn't ask themselves. They are jealous of their autonomy – which doesn't guarantee that they won't fall into the trap of less obvious dependencies. They no longer have to overcome certain obstacles which exhausted those women who went before them, but there are other obstacles which still have to be identified and confronted.

In all this, one thing is clear: women have begun to talk to each other, to meet and discuss things, to talk about their own experience. This is possibly a completely new historical phenomenon. Man is no longer the path that women have to tread.

Co-option

We have always thought that the danger of 'co-opting' the women's movement would come from its being absorbed into the system – any system whether politically left or right.

The first debate that influenced, nourished and also blocked feminism was its ideological (and practical) debate with Marxism. This debate, which pits the class struggle and women's struggle against each other, and which took up so many of our early meetings, seems less urgent today without actually ever being resolved, theoretically. This is probably because Marxist parties have been shaken by the denunciation of Stalinism and its repeated appearances, because their demand for unity in their 'orthodoxy' has been threatened, not only by people on the outside but from within, because people have begun to think for themselves again. But it has also been because of the clear vision and energy of many feminists on the left, who resisted the co-option of women's problems by the class struggle, and showed this resistance inside their party. The particularity of women's struggle – opposed and considered to be bourgeois deviation for so long – is no longer denied or totally ignored by parties on the left. These parties – or at least some of their leaders – have not given up, and are still developing their strategies of absorption in more subtle ways; but the question of the specific struggle of women has been raised and raised publicly. Marxist researchers are now trying to reappraise the relation of economic exploitation and gender exploitation without falling into an economistic approach.

On the other hand, reformism is equally dangerous. The movement's entry into institutional structures, through individual entry, meant running the risk of reducing or even eliminating its revolutionary nature. It was feared that specific political and legislative changes would allow those in power to defuse its demands. And that the women who participated in these structures – really, or as was more often the case, as tokens – played their game. That is why it seemed and still seems of major importance to us that specific spaces must be created and kept going on the edge of this system, spaces which resist the system and allow women to develop, in their truly radical nature, their thinking and their practice. This was, and remains, the meaning of the feminist movement.

But while this danger of reformism via 'entryism' remains present, it is not the most threatening to us, at least not at the moment. Patriarchy has benefited from letting women in. Such reforms as there are few and far between. They are feeble, and women are always in the minority and are always patronized. The system's conscious or unconscious self-defence strategy seems more subtle these days. It works through actively infiltrating and perverting 'marginality' itself. It doesn't push feminism towards a more 'serious', legal existence: it takes it as it is and turns it into a fashion, a consumer product, mostly cultural but also economic. Women become a new market. After an initial, violent rejection of feminism, patriarchy begins a many-sided attack on it, in order to make it less threatening. After misrepresenting and ostracizing it, it then decides to represent it and portray it in the media. This is when the cry of rage becomes an image, turned to mush by the news. Even in the most reactionary and sexist papers, they talk, everywhere, cheerfully, about rape or about battered women. But the medium is the message and it makes everything it touches banal. The aim is not to mobilize but to entertain. The aim is to level everything out via verbal inflation. Woman, in the shape of the 'new woman' is on the front page, the cover of magazines, subject of a publisher's series, cabaret shows, electoral speeches, university courses. On show, it sells things, brings audiences – however small.

And feminism itself seems to have changed, or is at least concerned to change, its image. The 1970s feminism, violent and negative, anti-men, is being replaced by feminism with a smiling face. This trend can be seen in two, possibly antagonistic, directions that feminism is taking: 'collaborative' feminism (with men), and ghetto feminism. It is as if it was important everywhere today to reassure and seduce by giving women, like men, a super-gratifying or triumphant image of themselves. Feminism has gone from dark to brightly-coloured, from war to celebration, from a T-shirt to a trendy blouse.

[Françoise Collin here moves to talk about the media that she calls parafeminist and how glossy, so-called feminist magazines give an image of feminism that eliminates struggle, differences and women's reality. She talks of how the militant journals of the early 1970s have been replaced by professional stylish magazines and how this is dangerous.]

When we thought we had given space to the informal, had liberated the spoken word, here was this liberation printed on a page, here the tape recorder and the video recorder taking it over and giving it a shape. By 'letting women speak out', in their different voices, we are solidifying them, making their voices sound the same, taming them.

Willingly or unwillingly, inevitably or avoidably, we may be accomplices in this travesty. As soon as we speak or write; as soon as we open a restaurant, a women's centre, a library; as soon as we organize a party, produce a film, a show, a book, a journal, a newspaper; as soon as we are happy or unhappy; as soon as we are seen and let ourselves be seen, we become part of this 'theatrical society' that manipulated us so well in the past. It is as if the more we speak and see, the more we are 'had', the more we have to stay in the shadows, take to the hills, become invisible and unreadable to escape it. It is as if a revolutionary existence is only possible in absolute secrecy, underground: a secrecy where groups still worked; women's groups at work, together silently; ants that maybe eat away at the earth; isolated thinkers but resistant in their actions.

Five years ago, it was enough that women spoke out, began to write, for it to be shocking. At that time, speaking or writing were revolutionary gestures, for oneself and for others; and certain words and certain questions were enough then to open discussion. This is no longer so. These words and these questions are often only stylistic devices. In the whole vague question of women, by and for women, we see the emergence of stereotypes, clichés, mannerisms.

How then can we speak or write, without falling into this? Where is our radicalism today? We are beginning to understand that for those men and women who are sick of words, throwing a bomb would sometimes seem to be the only pure gesture, the only expression which was not co-optable. But if we hate violence, then where is our gesture, where is this unused word, that inexhaustible word? Where is the cry that they can't turn into a chorus?

Some, many, women will say that this is a pessimistic vision. No one can deny the quantitively beneficial effects of diffusion by the media of whatever kind, of the increase in para- or pseudo-feminist groups – in short, co-option. The spreading of new ideas, even if the message is diluted, takes them to wider audiences and may at least reduce resistance to change. What radical actions and thoughts don't do may be done by less scrupulous others. And just as the media exploits and makes money out of the risky work of radicalism, so, by supreme cunning, radicalism can co-opt the effects of co-option, walk in its footsteps. We need a new strategy that will allow us to do this, and to work on people who are already informed and aware. Action would no longer be making a first contact, but going beyond that. Co-option in a way encourages and forces us to go further.

As we have said, the *cahiers du Grif* began at a time when there was no information (in French), either in the traditional or in the feminist press. At a time when, at least in Belgium, there was a demand, a demand by women, a demand which had no response. The *cahiers* was not a magazine like others, but was a group in constant contact, always ready to listen to collective and individual problems and voices. A heroic time, which we miss, of course, but a time which ate up our energy.

Today, the refinement and the development of the theoretical and practical problematic of feminism no longer permits this all-encompassing attitude. Work has become more specifically focused, even though it is still all-absorbing. Other people have taken on certain 'tasks' – such as women's centres, or information. We now have the chance to think, in a more precise way, about our own practice: where our demands are taking us, what our goals are. Surrounded by co-option and by the dilution of our ideas, our most pressing task is clearly to keep alive feminism's revolutionary will, with a more radical practice and a more radical voice. But what exactly is this radicalism? What are the shapes it takes, the paths it takes, for each of us? Is it time, now, for guerilla warfare or for retreat to a monastery? Is it time for action – and what action? Is it time for solitude or for being together? For autonomy or for subversive entryism?

After five years of communal experience and practice, the time, for us at least, is for re-finding ourselves and for thinking. We need to allow enjoyment and new ideas back into our lives, let our imaginations flow unrestrainedly, allow ourselves to be carried by friendships that we choose, place friendship ahead of the imperative of sympathy-with-everyone, and the un-reasoning disorder of desire ahead of activist order. This is only liberation in movement. We cannot allow ourselves to fossilize, even in success. We are indispensable, every woman is indispensable, but we are interchangeable.

Notes and references

Françoise Collin would like to add that this article represented a particular stage in her thinking, and that she has continued to develop and broaden her ideas.